People to Know

# Margaret Bourke-White
## Daring Photographer

Sara McIntosh Wooten

**Enslow Publishers, Inc.**

40 Industrial Road         PO Box 38
Box 398                     Aldershot
Berkeley Heights, NJ 07922   Hants GU12 6BP
USA                          UK
http://www.enslow.com

**Library of Congress Cataloging-in-Publication Data**

Wooten, Sara McIntosh.
    Margaret Bourke-White : daring photographer / Sara McIntosh Wooten.
        p. cm. — (People to know)
    Includes bibliographical references and index.
    ISBN 0-7660-1534-3
        1. Bourke-White, Margaret, 1904–1971—Juvenile literature. 2. Women photographers—United States—Biography—Juvenile literature. 3. Photographers— United States—Biography—Juvenile literature. [1. Bourke-White, Margaret, 1904–1971. 2. Photographers. 3. Women—Biography.] I. Title. II. Series.
    TR140.B6 W66 2002
    770'.92—dc21

                                                            2001007285

Printed in the United States of America

10 9 8 7 6 5 4 3 2 1

**To Our Readers:**
We have done our best to make sure all Internet Addresses in this book were active and appropriate when we went to press. However, the author and the publisher have no control over and assume no liability for the material available on those Internet sites or on other Web sites they may link to. Any comments or suggestions can be sent by e-mail to comments@enslow.com or to the address on the back cover.

Every effort has been made to locate all copyright holders of material used in this book. If any errors or omissions have occurred, corrections will be made in future editions of this book.

**Illustration Credits:** Margaret Bourke-White Papers, Department of Special Collections, Syracuse University Library; used with permission of the Estate of Margaret Bourke-White, pp. 12, 14, 17, 21, 24, 27, 33, 37, 47, 51, 58, 61, 71, 85; Margaret Bourke-White/Time Pix, pp. 8, 65, 92, 97; National Archives, pp. 4, 81.

**Cover Illustration:** Margaret Bourke-White Papers, Department of Special Collections, Syracuse University Library; used with permission of the Estate of Margaret Bourke-White.

# Contents

*Margaret Bourke-White*

# A Sinking Ship

All they felt was a dull thud in the middle of the night. No terrifying crash at all.[1] Yet, with that jolt, photographer Margaret Bourke-White knew immediately what had happened.[2] The troopship, on its way to North Africa carrying 6,400 British and American soldiers and nurses to battle in World War II, had just received a direct hit from a German torpedo. They were going down.

Bourke-White and her cabinmates, two Scottish nurses, jumped to their feet. The ship's electricity was knocked out by the blast, so they grabbed flashlights, then quickly dressed and put on their helmets. Within three minutes they were making their way through the narrow passageways, up the stairs, and onto the sharply listing deck. Bourke-White clutched her emergency bag. In it she had packed her smallest camera, some film, and several lenses. She left behind what she considered unnecessary—extra clothes and packets of food.[3]

There was no panic among the passengers. In silence, they moved into their assigned places. Everyone knew exactly what to do.[4] For the past five days the captain had insisted on two or three practice drills each day in case Germans attacked their ship.

Now their practice was paying off. As the thousands of nurses and soldiers poured onto the deck, the order to abandon ship was given. Everyone moved to the lifeboat stations and got in line to board. Everyone, that is, except Margaret Bourke-White. She was traveling with the massive troopship not as a nurse but as a photographer for *Life* magazine. She had received permission in advance to take pictures in the event of just such a crisis. This was the kind of dramatic photographic opportunity she liked.

But it was 2:00 A.M., and despite the brightness of the moon, there was not enough natural light for taking pictures. Suddenly, without a job to do, Bourke-White had no distraction from the fear and uncertainty that lay ahead.[5] The full seriousness of the situation hit, and Bourke-White turned her attention to her own safety.

She realized that her lifeboat might already have been loaded and launched.[6] Fighting the steep tilt of the sinking ship's deck, Bourke-White made her way to her assigned station. She arrived just as the British and American nurses were boarding.

Her relief soon turned to shock. As a member of Lifeboat 12, she climbed into the small boat only to find herself sitting waist deep in cold Mediterranean seawater. The torpedo's blast had showered water into the lifeboats, and no one was sure if they would even float.

Lifeboat 12 was lowered unsteadily onto the ocean's surface. Bourke-White later wrote down her impressions of the desperate scene. She described "hundreds of men scrambling to escape down rope nets flung over the side [of the ship]."[7] The water was filled with people struggling to swim or desperately clutching floating debris.

Bourke-White and the others soon found that their lifeboat's rudder was broken. That made it hard to escape the suction created by the sinking ship. The sea was churning wildly, and without the help of a rudder, the waves kept beating them back against the great ship's side. Once they finally managed to steer clear, those who were not overcome with sea-sickness took turns rowing or bailing water with their helmets.[8]

Meanwhile, other lifeboats joined the chaotic scene. One capsized just as it hit the water, spilling its occupants into the frigid sea. Some were lucky enough to swim to another boat; the others drowned.

The troopship had been one of a large convoy heading to North Africa. After the torpedo attack, the other ships scattered, abandoning their wounded

*The survivors in lifeboats sang and told jokes to keep their spirits up. At last they were rescued and taken aboard a nearby ship, above.*

sister ship. That way they might avoid becoming targets of German submarines and their torpedoes. Bourke-White and the other survivors were alone, drifting on the sea. As the night wore on, the moon set and the sinking troopship disappeared from view. How long would they remain adrift? How long could they last in this condition?

Bourke-White later described her experience that night as one of the most frightening of her life.[9] For her, that was quite a claim. Since beginning her career in photography fifteen years earlier, she had lived through adventure after adventure. She had survived the German bombs that destroyed Moscow. She had dangled from airplanes to take dramatic photos for advertisements. She had been lost in Antarctica, stranded in the frozen wastes with no radio contact. And before her career was over, she would undergo still more thrilling challenges in her work for *Life* magazine.

As with all her earlier brushes with disaster, Bourke-White would make her way out this time, too. Sometime after dawn on the day after the attack, a British flying boat sighted the little groups of survivors and signaled to a nearby destroyer. After eight hours, the occupants of Lifeboat 12 were rescued. They were deposited that night in the port city of Algiers on the northwest coast of Africa. Bourke-White was safe once again, and ready for her next assignment.

# "Reject the Easy Path!"

Margaret Bourke-White was born on June 14, 1904, in the Bronx, New York. She was the second child in the White household. Her sister, Ruth, was three years old.

Soon after Margaret's birth, the Whites moved to Bound Brook, New Jersey. They lived in a large, comfortable house there, surrounded by trees and open fields. The Watchung Mountains were within walking distance.

Margaret's parents, Joseph White and Minnie Bourke, were an unusual couple. With a religious zeal, they held strong beliefs about life. Above all, Joseph and Minnie were perfectionists. They believed in striving for excellence. They lived with a steely will to do the very best at everything they attempted.[1]

Margaret's parents scorned ease and comfort.

Instead, they felt that true joy was to be found in hard work, high standards, and the determination to stay with a job until it was finished. As their family grew, they remained steadfast in passing those beliefs on to their children. The results of their efforts would have far-reaching effects on their daughter Margaret.

Joseph White was an engineer and inventor. He worked for a company that made printing presses. Handsome, with black hair and dark eyes, Mr. White was a man of few words. He spent hours at a time in concentrated thought about his work. The printing press was his love, and he devoted his waking hours to coming up with ideas to improve it.

The rest of the family did everything they could to encourage and respect their father's thinking time. On Sundays, while Joseph was deep in thought, the rest of the family tiptoed around so as not to disturb him. Sometimes, when the family went to a restaurant to eat, Joseph would spend the entire time silently working out a printing problem in his mind. The family would watch him scribble notes on the tablecloth. When dinner was over they would leave, although Joseph had not even touched his food.[2]

Minnie Bourke, Margaret's mother, was an independent woman. A devoted wife and mother, she was constantly striving to improve herself and her children.[3] She wanted them to challenge themselves and develop their abilities as much as possible. They later remembered that she often criticized them as she tried to make them the best they could be. To encourage

*Margaret said her mother was "a born teacher." Minnie Bourke often read to her children and expected them to excel in school.*

their stamina and build strength of character she would say, "Reject the easy path! Do it the hard way!"[4]

Margaret was an obedient child, and she tried hard to please her parents.[5] Still, from time to time she went through difficult phases. Like many small children, she was afraid of the dark. She was also fearful of being alone, especially at night. But Margaret's parents did not believe in fear.[6] Instead, they prized courage, and Minnie Bourke devised a plan to help her daughter overcome her fright. At night she would take Margaret outside and make a game of seeing who could run faster. Each evening, Minnie increased the distance just a bit. Finally, Margaret became comfortable in the dark.

To help Margaret get used to being by herself, her parents would leave the house each evening after she went to bed. They were just going for a little walk, and Margaret knew they would be back soon. But each night they stayed out a little longer. One night they were gone for four hours. But by this time, Margaret was so trusting that while they were out, she peacefully went to sleep. Her fear of being by herself was over. Her mother's games helped Margaret develop a confidence that would last throughout her life.

As their children grew, the Whites frowned on any activities they considered frivolous. The children were rarely allowed to go to the movies. Chewing gum and reading comics (known as "funny papers") were forbidden. Nor could they play cards or wear fancy clothes. To the Whites, life was serious business.

Among their many interests, Margaret's parents were avid naturalists. They loved being outdoors observing and learning about insect and animal life. Some of Margaret's fondest memories were of taking long walks with her father in the woods near their home.[7] Together they would silently observe the wildlife. He would teach his daughter about nature. She learned which snakes were poisonous, which were harmless, and how to pick them up and hold them without fear. He taught her about turtles and insects, and how to identify and mimic various bird calls.

Minnie encouraged her daughter's interest in the outdoors by allowing all sorts of creatures into their home as pets or science experiments. Besides rabbits and hamsters, Margaret had two turtles, Attila and Alaric, who made their home under the piano. She also brought home a continual assortment of frogs,

*Margaret and her older sister, Ruth, were not afraid of heights. They often paraded across the top of a fence on the way to school.*

moths, and butterflies. Once she fed and cared for a collection of two hundred caterpillars. She kept them under rows of overturned water glasses and jars on the dining room windowsill.

Garter snakes were common among the White menagerie, too. The family even kept a baby boa constrictor for a time. But one of the household favorites was a hognose snake, also called a puff adder. The harmless creature entertained the Whites and their friends. First he would inflate his neck and hiss wildly. Then he would roll on his belly and play dead. On Sunday afternoons, the tame snake often slept in Mrs. White's lap as she read the newspaper in front of the fireplace.

Another hobby Joseph White introduced his daughter to was photography. She helped him develop his pictures in the darkroom they set up in their bathroom. Over the years Joseph took thousands of pictures of his family, his work, and nature, often experimenting with light and with different camera lenses and cameras. Many of his photographs were displayed on the walls of their home.

When the time came for Margaret to begin her formal education, she attended a four-room school in Bound Brook with her sister, Ruth. They made a game of walking to the little neighborhood schoolhouse every day, balancing like acrobats on top of the board fences that ran along their route. When Margaret was seven, her brother, Roger, was born. With his arrival, the family was complete.

At school, Margaret showed a natural flair for

drama. She enjoyed the effect she created by casually entering the schoolhouse with her pet hognose snake draped across her arm. The reaction she received from her classmates gave her the attention she craved.

Margaret was eight years old when her father introduced her to the world of machines. They fascinated him, and he wanted to pass that love and fascination on to Margaret. One day he took her with him to visit a foundry, a factory where metal machine parts are made from molten steel. Inside, parts of his printing presses were being created.

The foundry was filled with overwhelming heat, energy, and power. Margaret felt special just being there, particularly in the company of the father she adored.[8] As she watched the giant ladles pour the molten metal into the molds, Margaret was transfixed. On that day her love affair with machines began. Later she would describe her fascination with the experience as a "sudden magic of flowing metal and flying sparks."[9] Her sense of wonder at the power and beauty of machinery would last her lifetime. It would also lead her into the career that would make her famous.

But as a young girl, Margaret did not know that her future lay in photography. When she was ten years old, she wanted to be a herpetologist—a scientist who studies snakes. She dreamed of becoming world famous and traveling to distant lands.

Margaret knew it was an unusual choice of careers, especially for a woman. For her, that only

*Eleven-year-old Margaret rescued this baby bird and befriended its father. Margaret held the tiny creature as it was being fed.*

added to its appeal. Even at that early age, Margaret would say she wanted "[to do] all the things that women never do."[10] Her parents' efforts at developing her self-confidence and independence had paid off.

When it came time for high school, Margaret—or "Peg," as she was called then—attended nearby Plainfield High School. During her four years there she worked hard at her studies, just as her parents expected. She was an excellent student. Her specialties were English and biology. She also found time to participate in a number of extracurricular activities. She joined the Debating Club and was an editor of the Plainfield High School yearbook. She also followed through with her love of drama, acting in various school plays and serving as president of the Dramatic Club. Sports attracted Margaret, too. She liked swimming, basketball, and hockey.

In the tenth grade, Margaret entered a school contest for the best eight-hundred-word original story. Margaret put off writing her entry until the last possible moment. Just two hours before the deadline, she sat down on her porch step and hurriedly scribbled out a story. It was about a boy who wanted a dog. While she wrote, a friend sat beside her helping to keep count of her words. Even though she was competing against other tenth-, eleventh-, and twelfth-graders, Margaret won first place in the contest. The prize was $15 worth of books. Her choices were unusual but not surprising; she wanted a book on frogs, a book on moths, and a book on reptiles.

Despite her close family ties and many interests,

Margaret was lonely in high school. She craved the romantic attention of boys her age. She had plenty of male friends, but no dates. Margaret loved to dance, and she dreamed of being asked to a high school dance. When she won the writing contest, she was sure that honor would lead to a dance invitation. But her hopes were dashed. Although that would all change once she got to college, Margaret's deep hurt that no boy asked her to a dance would continue throughout her high school years.[11]

# Rough Waters

As soon as she graduated from Plainfield High School, Margaret turned her sights toward her college education. She still wanted to be a herpetologist.[1] She enrolled at Columbia University in New York City, starting classes in the fall of 1921.

Just four months later, tragedy struck the White family. On January 17, 1922, Joseph White suffered a massive stroke. He died the next day. Deep into her classes, Margaret hardly had a chance to mourn the loss of the father she loved so much. She decided to take a course in photography. Working with cameras reminded her of her father, so it was a way to keep her link with him alive.[2]

In 1922, photography was coming into its own as a science, an art, and a hobby. A great debate

*"I simply adored him," said Margaret of her father, above. She described him as "very artistic."*

raged among artists and photographers: Should photography be viewed as art, or was it a technical craft? Many photographers were experimenting with techniques to soften and blur the edges of the subjects in their photographs, making the photos look more like paintings.

Margaret's photography course at Columbia was taught by Clarence H. White, a master photographer of the time. White was among those who thought photography was a form of art. He was also a brilliant teacher and gave Margaret a strong foundation in modern design.[3]

Clarence White's philosophy of excellence fit right in with Margaret's family training. Speaking of him, she wrote, "You somehow absorbed from him that feeling that any picture that was important enough to make was one that the photographer should work on until he had made it as perfect as he could possibly make it."[4] Their shared passion for perfection would pay off for Margaret down the road.

That summer, Margaret needed a job. Money was tight in the household after her father's death. No one was quite sure how Margaret would be able to continue her education. But she put her newly acquired photographic skills to use. She found a job working as a camp counselor at Camp Agaming on Lake Bantam in Connecticut. She was hired to take camp pictures and work with the campers as a nature counselor.

Margaret worked hard getting shots of camp. True to her nature, she was a perfectionist. If she wanted a picture of Lake Bantam, she might stay up all night to get the right image of the sun as it burst over the lake at dawn. And if the light was not right that morning, or there was a mist or fog, she would stay up the next night and the next if need be. She did whatever was necessary to get the effect she wanted in her photographs.

That summer Margaret also began another practice she would become known for as an adult. To get the shot she was after, she began to take physical risks without concern for her safety. Once, after a hike to the top of a mountain, Margaret wanted a bird's-eye photograph from the top. She climbed across a barricade and hung over the side of a sheer drop so she could photograph the valley in the distance below.

Margaret also became a businesswoman. To make more money, she set up her own photography business selling picture postcards of the camp. She also took portraits of many of the campers and their cabins. The campers were eager to buy her photographs and send them home to their parents.

Then Margaret had another idea for her popular photos. She decided to see if storekeepers in the nearby towns would be interested in buying her postcards to sell to tourists. After visiting some local shop owners, she ended up with more orders than she had dreamed possible.[5] By the end of the summer, Margaret had printed nearly two thousand postcards.

Yet even with her financial success that summer, she still did not have enough money to pay for another year of college. Then Margaret got some unexpected help. One day in September she got a call from a man named Mr. Munger. He invited her to stop by his home for a visit. Munger lived in Bound Brook with his unmarried sister. Both were elderly and interested in helping promising students fund their college educations. A friend had given him Margaret's name.

The Mungers interviewed Margaret and learned of her plans to become a herpetologist. Impressed by her energy and intelligence, they agreed to pay for her next year's education. They considered her an investment. She would not need to pay the money back; she could return their kindness by helping someone

*Margaret enrolled at the University of Michigan with plans to become a herpetologist, a scientist studying snakes.*

else one day. In the meantime, they would pay for everything—room, board, tuition, books, supplies, and even clothes if she needed them.

Less than two weeks later, Margaret's education plans were back on track. This time she began classes at the University of Michigan in Ann Arbor. It had a well-known program in herpetology.

Soon Margaret experienced another profound change in her life. She found herself at the center of attention from male students. At dances, she no longer had to worry. Young men were practically lining up to dance with her.

At the university, Margaret continued taking pictures. She kept a camera with her constantly. She worked as a photographer for the school yearbook, taking photos of campus buildings and school events. The idea began to creep into her mind that perhaps she should make a career of photography, rather than herpetology.[6]

As the semester wore on, Margaret's popularity increased. One day, she caught the eye of a handsome senior, Everett Chapman. As she was entering the cafeteria through its revolving door, he was leaving. Noticing Margaret, he decided to hold her captive until she agreed to a date. They went round and round in the revolving door until he finally got his wish. As Bourke-White later remembered the day, it was love at first sight for them both.[7]

Everett Chapman, nicknamed "Chappie," was an electrical engineering major. He was a solid student who worked hard and made good grades. He and

Margaret found they had all sorts of interests in common, and had lots of fun when they were together. And although Chappie was more talkative, his intense concentration in his work reminded Margaret of her father.[8]

That spring, Chappie proposed marriage to Margaret. That created some problems. Margaret was young, just eighteen years old. She was wild about Chappie, but she was not ready to get married. She wanted to experience all the fun and attention she had dreamed about for so long. Margaret also worried that marriage might bring an abrupt end to her ambitious career plans.[9] Chappie was insistent, and Margaret did not know what to do.

That summer the couple parted, each going home to work at a summer job. They returned to the university in the fall, and the tensions between them continued to mount. Chappie drifted into black moods whenever his feelings were hurt. Sometimes he refused to talk to Margaret for hours. He suffered raging fits of jealousy and became demanding of her every moment's attention. Margaret met his fits with tears and hysteria. It was an emotional roller coaster for them both.

Early in 1924, the couple decided to plan a June wedding, hoping that marriage would settle all the tensions between them. On June 13, 1924, Margaret became Mrs. Everett Chapman. With no extra money to spend on the ceremony, Margaret wore a borrowed dress, shoes, and stockings. The wedding ring, which Chappie had made, broke into two pieces the night

*"Chappie" had many of the same interests as Margaret, including photography.*

before. They had to use a borrowed ring for the ceremony.

The next day, rather than begin their honeymoon, the Chapmans went back to work. They had photos to develop that would bring them some much-needed cash. A week later, the newlyweds headed off for their wedding trip. They drove seventeen miles to a lakeside cottage that Chappie's parents owned.

But more trouble loomed. Within two days, Chappie's mother and sister arrived at the cottage, along with their suitcases. They were joining Chappie and his new wife on their honeymoon. It did not take long for Mrs. Chapman to show her hatred and jealousy of her new daughter-in-law. Margaret realized that Mrs. Chapman had overly strong emotional ties to her son and that she would do her best to destroy his marriage.[10]

Despite problems, the marriage limped along for two years. In the fall of 1924, the couple moved to Lafayette, Indiana, where Chappie had taken a job teaching at Purdue University. Margaret enrolled to take up her studies once again. She was beginning as a freshman for the third time. That year was a lonely one for Margaret. She was the wife of a professor, and other students her age shied away from her. At the same time, the other professors' wives were much older than she. It was a difficult time.[11]

The next year, the Chapmans moved to Cleveland, Ohio. Chappie had taken a job at Lincoln Electric Company. Margaret worked at Cleveland's Museum of Natural History teaching public school students. At night she took classes at Case Western Reserve University. By this time she had changed her major to education. As her marriage continued on rocky ground, she knew she could find a job as a teacher if she needed to support herself.

Margaret left Chappie the next year. Later, she looked back on the whole experience without bitterness. She wrote that after the "loneliness and the anguish . . . nothing would ever seem so hard again."[12]

Leaving Cleveland, Margaret enrolled at Cornell University in Ithaca, New York, where she would finally complete her degree. She chose Cornell because of its good biology program and its picturesque waterfalls. While at Cornell, Margaret once again turned to photography. She took photos of the campus towers, halls, and dormitories, and, as before, she found that people wanted to buy her work.[13] The *Cornell Alumni News* featured her campus photos regularly on its covers. Margaret would later write of the camera's "growing feeling of rightness" in her hands.[14]

During Easter vacation in 1927, Margaret decided she needed an objective, professional opinion of her photographic work. Did she have talent enough to make photography a career? She had to find out before she could commit herself to that direction. Margaret sought advice at the architectural firm of York and Sawyer in New York City. A friend had recommended one of their architects, Benjamin Moskowitz, as a good judge of talent.

Margaret ventured into the firm's offices late one afternoon. Under her arm she carried her portfolio filled with samples of her photographs. As the elevator opened onto Moskowitz's floor, she came upon Moskowitz. He was on his way out, but she introduced herself and told him what she wanted. As he listened politely, he edged toward the elevator and pressed the down button.

Her spirits were dampened by this brush-off, but Margaret did not stop. In the few seconds before the elevator arrived, she quickly opened her portfolio. The photograph she displayed was from the top of Cornell's library tower, showing the river below as viewed through the tower's grillwork. She had climbed that tower again and again at dawn to get just the lighting she wanted.

The elevator came . . . and went away empty. Moskowitz was impressed. He ushered Margaret back into his office and called for his colleagues to take a look at her work. She left the offices of York and Sawyer that afternoon with the assurance that she did have the talent to become an architectural photographer.[15]

With that, Margaret faced the future with hope. Her marriage had ended, but now it seemed as though her life was just beginning.

# A Career Is Launched

With her diploma from Cornell tightly in hand and her career direction set, Margaret was poised for the future. She decided to move back to Cleveland and open her first photography studio. At the same time, she began using the hyphenated last name of Bourke-White, combining her mother's maiden name with her father's last name. She thought it would stand out, and that would be a help in her business.[1]

Armed with high hopes and her portfolio, Bourke-White hit the pavement looking for work. She made the rounds of Cleveland's architectural firms, hoping to be hired to photograph buildings they had designed.

Soon after her arrival, Bourke-White was in downtown Cleveland when she happened upon an unusual scene. In the middle of Cleveland's Public Square, an elderly man stood on a soapbox, arms outstretched, preaching with all his might. But no one was paying any attention. His audience consisted of a flock of city pigeons scurrying to find bits of food on the pavement.

Bourke-White thought the scene would make a unique photograph, but she had no camera with her. She raced to a nearby camera store and begged the clerk to lend her one. Emerging from the store she stopped again, this time to buy a bag of peanuts. Back at the square, she tossed peanuts to the pigeons to keep them busy on the ground and then began snapping the scene. The result would be Bourke-White's first commercially sold photograph. Cleveland's Chamber of Commerce bought it for the cover of *The Clevelander*, its magazine promoting the city.[2]

That day had another bonus. When she returned the camera to the shop, she learned that the clerk, Alfred Hall Bemis, was an expert photographer. He became Bourke-White's mentor in Cleveland. Over the next three years he would give her technical advice, lend her equipment, and roll up his sleeves to help with developing when she needed an extra pair of hands. She would always be grateful, later writing that "one would need ten others to replace a single Bemis."[3]

As she continued to look for work, Bourke-White was especially concerned about presenting a professional image. She knew it would be tough getting male clients to take her seriously as a photographer and

*When Bourke-White saw this scene, she knew she had to photograph it. The picture is titled* A Preacher and His Parishioners, Cleveland, 1928.

businesswoman. She owned only one suit, a gray one, which she wore with either a blue hat and gloves, or a red hat and gloves. Each evening when she returned to her little studio apartment, she would record on note cards which companies she had visited that day, whom she had spoken with, and which outfit she had worn. Bourke-White wanted to be sure to wear a different outfit if she returned to a company for a second visit.

At that time, architectural photography was an unusual career for a woman. Bourke-White was immersed in a male-dominated world of architects and businessmen. But she made the most of her situation. With stylishly cut hair and fashionable high heels, along with hat and gloves, Bourke-White made a unique impression. Most important, her portfolio of work revealed her talents as a photographer.

Before long, Bourke-White landed her first assignment. An architectural firm, Pitkin and Mott, needed a photograph of a new school they had designed. She went to the site and studied the building from every angle. She decided to shoot the school at dawn with the sun's rays coming over the building. For four days she was up before dawn and at the site, ready to shoot. But each time the sunrise was not clear enough to suit her. Finally, she got the lighting she wanted. But when the photos were developed, she discovered a new problem. The building had not been landscaped yet. No trees, bushes, or flowers had been planted to break the expanse of mud and debris that surrounded the school.

Bourke-White ran to a nearby florist and bought

bunches of asters. Then she stuck the cut stems into the ground in front of the school to create an instant, though temporary, flower bed. The final shot, taken from the ground looking up, showed the new school looking friendly and ready for students with its bright fringe of flowers. The photograph was a success and later appeared in *Architecture* magazine.

That job was followed by a string of others. Most required Bourke-White to photograph buildings or houses. The architects who had designed them wanted to advertise their work. Sometimes wealthy families hired her to photograph their estates. With her apartment as her studio, she developed her film at night in her kitchen sink and rinsed the photos in her bathtub.

Bourke-White's job as a professional photographer was awkward and painstaking. For a shoot, she often equipped herself with as many as five cameras, along with flashbulbs, film, and several lenses. Cameras were much bigger and heavier in those days. Most had to be mounted on a twenty-pound tripod, which she also lugged along. And with her passion for perfection, it was not unusual for Bourke-White to take an entire day to get the one picture she wanted.

As her business began to expand, Bourke-White's photographic style began to change as well. By this time, the winds of opinion had shifted in the photographic world. Rather than making photos look like paintings with the use of soft-focus techniques, photography had turned to realism. The new emphasis was on sharply focused photographs that would affirm what the camera was designed to do. Bourke-White picked up the trend and would continue with it throughout her career.

Through 1927 and into 1928, Bourke-White concentrated on getting her photography business off the ground. But as time wore on she became dissatisfied with her direction. Taking photographs of buildings and estates was fine, but she realized they were not her passion. What she really wanted to do was industrial photography. She could not forget the thrill she had felt when her father had taken her to visit the foundry.[4] The fascination with heavy industry still gripped her heart. Now that she was a photographer, she wanted more than anything else to capture the magic of industry in photographs. Later in an interview she explained, "In the simple black-and-white truthfulness of the photograph, the story of the machine and the worker who operates it can best be told."[5]

Her timing could not have been better. In 1928, American industry had risen to a peak of productivity and profits. The nation saw industry as its path to prosperity, a symbol for unlimited opportunity. Bourke-White saw the camera, with its directness and mechanical nature, as the perfect tool to record machines.[6]

Her problem was how to break into industrial photography. As a woman, it would be especially difficult. Industry was considered a man's world. It was dirty and crude, not to mention dangerous. The deafening roar inside a factory was enough to fluster the timid.

Anyone could get hurt wandering through a factory, and it was not considered a proper place for a woman.

Cleveland's heavy industry was centered in an area called the Flats. Connected to downtown Cleveland by high bridges crossing the Cuyahoga River, the Flats was crisscrossed by a maze of railroad tracks and freight trains. With giant smokestacks, tall cranes, blast furnaces, mountains of iron ore, and barges making their way downriver, this concentrated area of factories and commerce was a dark and dirty place. But Bourke-White thought it was beautiful. To her, it was a place of purpose; it represented America's future.[7]

*With her photographs, Bourke-White earned enough money to purchase her first car, which she named Patrick.*

Bourke-White knew the Flats was where her photographic future lay. Like a magnet, it pulled her. Any time she was not shooting photographs or developing film for her paying clients, she found herself walking around the Flats, studying the movement and productivity. She began photographing the area, using every spare dime to buy film.

Bourke-White was not the first photographer drawn to the Flats. But where others chose to take panoramic shots, she did the opposite. Her photographs took the viewer right into the Flats for a close-up experience. Her shots isolated various parts of the district, creating a direct connection between the viewer and the photograph.[8]

The Otis Steel Company's huge buildings became her primary target. She knew what she would find inside, and she wanted to get the dynamic, powerful process of steelmaking recorded on film.[9] But women were not welcome inside Otis Steel.[10] Company officials did not want a woman to get hurt in the oppressive heat with heavy machinery in action. Not only that, they said, a woman's presence would distract the workers, putting them in potential danger. As a woman, she needed special permission just to get into the foundry—and would have to obtain additional authorization to take photographs. Bourke-White burned with her dilemma.

Finally, one of her clients arranged for her to meet with Elroy Kulas, president of Otis Steel. She explained her interest in taking photographs of the steelmaking process. She showed him her portfolio of industrial photographs. But Kulas remained skeptical. The last woman he had allowed inside the steel mill had fainted from the intense heat. Bourke-White assured him she was not the fainting kind.[11]

Bourke-White was not one to take no for an answer. She told him that it is the "power and vitality in industry that makes it a magnificent subject for photography."[12] By the time the interview was over, she had persuaded Kulas to let her inside the foundry to take her photographs. In the meantime, he was off on an extended trip to Europe.

Bourke-White had taken a giant step toward fulfilling her dream. Full of hope and excitement, she started to work. Kulas had given her full access to the steel mill, and it did not take her long to make herself at home. She wrote, "I would come into the steel mills, into the riot of flying sparks, rushing metal, bursts of smoke, and feel as though I were coming home, it seemed so much a part of me."[13]

Getting her photos sometimes meant getting in the way. And she was often working in dangerous conditions. Doing her job the way she wanted required climbing ladders and balancing precariously on scaffolding. Once, her camera's varnish bubbled into blisters from the overwhelming heat of the foundry's monstrous furnaces. The mill workers were distracted by the sight of a woman climbing fearlessly throughout their work areas. They were also concerned for her safety. She wrote, "[Men] think they must keep me from so-called 'danger,' and, of course, unless I can go where that is, I can't often get my picture."[14]

Mindful of the danger but unconcerned, Bourke-White continued her work, happy to be able to shoot her photos. But she soon found that her problems had just begun. At that time, no one had ever taken the kind of pictures she was after—and for good reason. Photographic equipment was not advanced enough.[15] Inside the foundry, there simply was not enough light to create printable photographs. Bourke-White took photograph after photograph on her first visits, only to develop the film and find, to her bitter disappointment, that it was unprintable. She realized she was in over her head.

She turned to her friend Alfred Bemis and his assistant, Earl Leiter, from the camera shop. Could they help her tackle this photographic challenge? Each day Bourke-White would continue her work for her paying clients. But her nights belonged to Otis Steel. Night after night, she returned to the foundry with Bemis and Leiter, each time bringing more equipment from the shop. They tried floodlights, different cables, flash powder, faster lenses. Nothing worked. The challenge was exhausting and exciting at the same time. They refused to give up.

One day a traveling salesman visited the camera shop. He was on his way to Hollywood, California, to sell a new lighting product, magnesium flares, to the movie industry. Perhaps the magnesium flares would provide the light they so desperately needed. Bourke-White and Bemis persuaded the salesman to let them try his flares in the steel mill.

With eleven flares blazing, they had enough light at last. Bourke-White was able to get the photographs she had dreamed about. She took pictures of liquid steel bubbling in its ladles with orange smoke rising above it. One photograph captured the paths of the sparks as they leapt from the fiery liquid.

When Kulas got back to Cleveland, Bourke-White nervously prepared to show him the results of her efforts.[16] She need not have worried. Kulas was amazed at what she had done, calling it "pioneering work."[17] He purchased eight of her prints for $100 each. That was ten times her normal fee. And he asked for eight more. They would appear in a company booklet, *The Story of Steel,* and would be featured in magazines and newspapers all over the Midwest. They would also pave Bourke-White's path to even greater success.

Bourke-White's work began to get attention. With her industrial photographs, she was breaking new ground. The *New York Sun* carried an article about her, titled "Dizzy Heights Have No Terror for This Girl Photographer, Who Braves Numerous Perils to Film the Beauty of Iron and Steel."[18] Her advertising photographs began appearing in national magazines, and *Architectural Record* published some of her industrial photos in 1929. Not surprisingly, her business expanded as her reputation grew.

Bourke-White was finally able to move her studio from her apartment into an office building. She chose Cleveland's most dramatic building, the newly constructed Terminal Tower. It was the city's tallest skyscraper. She hired a secretary and a technician to assist her in her work.

As Bourke-White's industrial photographs became known, her signature style began to stand out as well. Typically, a Bourke-White photo would show action of some kind, such as steam billowing above smokestacks, red-hot molten steel pouring from a gigantic two-hundred-ton ladle, or sparks shooting like fireworks into the blackness. She also learned to show contrasting elements that added drama to her photographs. She would look for compositions highlighting light against dark, old against new, smooth against rough. She wanted her photography to capture the energy and dynamic spirit of a factory, not just the machinery. With Bourke-White's vision, photographs of industry were transformed into works of art.

# Fame with *Fortune*

Early in 1929, Henry R. Luce, the young and highly successful publisher of *Time* magazine, saw Bourke-White's Otis Steel photographs in a midwestern newspaper. Soon afterward, he sent her a telegram inviting her to New York for an interview.

Bourke-White was perplexed.[1] Why would Luce think she might be interested in working for *Time*? It was a newsmagazine with few photographs. She was doing exactly what she wanted to do right there in Cleveland. Her business and future were broadening daily. Still, she decided a free trip to New York City would be nice. And while there, she could pursue new contacts that might lead to more business.[2]

Bourke-White soon learned the reason for Henry

Luce's invitation. He was not going to ask her to work for *Time*. He was planning a new monthly magazine about business and industry in America. The magazine would convey industry's dignity, beauty, and excitement.[3] Photography and text would be equal partners, and Luce wanted the magazine to feature dramatic views of the industrial world.[4] For its photographer, he wanted Margaret Bourke-White.

The job was tailor-made for Bourke-White. A whole new path suddenly opened up for her. Not wanting to be tied down to one employer, she agreed to work part-time for the new magazine, which was to be called *Fortune*. The rest of her time she would spend in Cleveland as a freelance photographer.

*Fortune*'s first issue was scheduled to appear on newsstands in February 1930. The feature article would be illustrated with Bourke-White's photos, but what should it be about? *Fortune* wanted an attention grabber about an industry that was important in the United States. The editors decided on the Swift and Company meatpacking plant in Chicago. Bourke-White's job would be to photograph the billion-dollar hog butchering and processing business.

Bourke-White was delighted with the unusual challenge.[5] In her photos of the meatpacking plant, she used repeating patterns to symbolize productivity and mass production. Through her camera's lenses, thousands of hogs in their pens became an expanse of gracefully curving backs. Another shot showed rows of hogs strung up by their rear hooves.

On the last day of the shoot, she photographed the

final stage of the process. Swift and Company was famous for saying that it used "all of the pig but the squeal."[6] The only part of the animal that was left over was called pig dust. Mountains of this dust were then mixed with hog feed for the next round of hogs.

The problem was the odor of the pig dust. The stench was so powerful that the editor from *Fortune* ran straight out to wait in the car—where he kept the windows tightly closed. But Bourke-White waded right in, setting up her camera and going to work. Her mounds of pig dust resembled graceful dunes of sand, a beautiful finish for the photographic essay.

With her work at Swift completed, Bourke-White began packing up her cameras to head home. The camera cloth and light cords had absorbed the disgusting packing house odors and could never be used again. She decided to leave them at the plant, along with instructions that they be burned.

Three months before *Fortune*'s first issue was published, the stock market crash of 1929 enveloped America in gloom and signaled the beginning of the Great Depression. At the time, Bourke-White was doing a shoot inside a bank in Boston, completely oblivious to the disaster unfolding around her. The question was, should *Fortune* continue with its publication plans in the face of such ominous signs? Luce chose to go forward.

His decision proved to be a good one. Despite the nation's failing economy, *Fortune* became known for publishing the finest photographs of any magazine in the country. Becoming the magazine's star photographer propelled Bourke-White to national fame. The *Fortune* assignments also expanded her experience. She now had the opportunity to cover a wide variety of industries and to travel more. For *Fortune,* Bourke-White covered such varied business-es as shoemaking, glassblowing, orchid growing, and fishing. Her childhood dream of an exotic career involving travel had come true. She was doing things that women had never done. And she was loving it.[7]

In the winter of 1929, New York City sponsored a contest for the highest building in the world. One contestant was the Chrysler Building. The Chrysler Corporation hired Bourke-White to photograph the skyscraper as it was being built. When it was almost finished, Bourke-White took on some of her most dar-ing work. Riding a hoist eight hundred feet above the sidewalk, often in freezing weather, she braved the building's highest tower to get her photographs. Not surprisingly, rather than fearing heights, she was attracted to them.[8] She was particularly fond of the building's stainless-steel gargoyles, which jutted out from the sixty-first floor. Sometimes she inched onto the back of a gargoyle to shoot the panoramic view of the city below.

Bourke-White fell in love with the Chrysler Building. After commuting between Cleveland and New York City for two years, she finally closed her Cleveland studio. She opened a new one, this time in the glamorous Chrysler Building itself, right beside one of the gargoyles. With her studio decorated in the latest styles, Bourke-White had an aquarium built

*For Bourke-White, capturing the perfect shot often meant taking risks. Here, balanced atop a gargoyle on the sixty-first floor of the Chrysler Building, she prepares to photograph the New York City skyline.*

into one wall. She also brought several tortoises and two alligators there as pets. They spent most of their time outside on the terrace.

To finance her extravagant new office, Bourke-White depended increasingly on the high-paying advertising business. Goodyear and Buick became two of her biggest clients. She increased her staff from two to eight. Between her advertising clients and her work at *Fortune,* Bourke-White was having the time of her life. She had made it in a man's profession, and her future looked bright.

# 6

# Pictures from Russia

On June 20, 1930, Bourke-White boarded the S.S. *Bremen* for Germany. *Fortune* was sending her there to photograph the new industries that were springing up throughout the country. The Germans were rebuilding after all the destruction they had suffered during World War I.

While in Germany, Bourke-White wanted to extend her assignment. She was determined to venture into the Soviet Union with her cameras. It had been thirteen years since the Communist Revolution had turned Russia's government upside down. The Russian monarchy had ended and a new Communist government was in place. Josef Stalin had become the leader of the Soviet Union.

When Stalin came to power, he controlled a country of 150 million people. Most were farmers, working the land as they had done for centuries. But Stalin wanted to make the Soviet Union a modern industrial power.

In 1928, under Stalin's orders, the Soviet Union began the first of a series of programs called Five-Year Plans. During the next five years he would turn the country's economy around, putting industry before agriculture. No country in history had made such a dramatic change so quickly. America's shift to industry had taken fifty years. But Stalin wanted the Soviets to catch up with other modern nations of the world.

Under the first of the Five-Year Plans, the Soviet people were forced to change lifestyles almost overnight. Millions of citizens were uprooted from the countryside and relocated into cities. They began building factories and railroads at a furious pace. Those left in the country were resettled on huge collective farms. Their job was to produce enough food to feed the rest of the country.

It was a harsh period of transition and millions would die from starvation or violence.[1] But for Bourke-White, the Soviet Union was being transformed into a wonderland of industry-in-progress. It was the perfect place for her to work. She wrote, "I wanted to go to Russia where all these industries would be new. I was eager to see what a factory would be like that had been plunged suddenly into being."[2]

*Fortune* was happy that Bourke-White wanted to try to get into the Soviet Union. But the editors doubted she would be given permission to enter the country.

No foreigners had been allowed there to take photographs since the Revolution.[3] But as Bourke-White would later write, "Nothing attracts me like a closed door."[4]

Bourke-White had applied for a visa from the Soviet officials before leaving for Germany. She was encouraged by the official who helped her. After seeing samples of her industrial photographs and hearing of her mission there, he told her, "Your pictures will be your passport."[5]

When Bourke-White arrived in Berlin, no visa awaited her at the Soviet embassy. Still, she was hopeful. "I knew that if the Soviet Government found me useful, they would smooth out some of the obstacles in my path."[6] Bourke-White's efforts finally got results. After nearly six weeks of waiting in Germany, her visa arrived at the Soviet embassy in Berlin. She would soon be on her way.

Immediately, she began preparing for the journey. She had heard that food would be scarce in the Soviet Union. Along with eight hundred pounds of camera equipment, she also filled a trunk with cheese, chocolate, sausages, and canned fruit and baked beans. Then she boarded the trans-Siberian train for Moscow.

Bourke-White found conditions in Moscow bleak. Deposited at the railroad station, she could find no taxis to take her and her mounds of luggage to her hotel. Finally, she hired a *droshky* (horse-drawn carriage), which she later described as "so worn it seemed a breath would blow it to pieces."[7] One Soviet advised, "Tell her that we are sorry things are so poor, but if she will come back in five years everything will be better."[8]

To travel throughout the country as she wanted, Bourke-White needed the Soviet government's permission. As with her visa, getting permission was not easy or quick. While she waited, she photographed the factories around Moscow, taking shots of bread factories, workers' clubs, and textile mills where cotton lace was made.

At last Bourke-White received a packet of official papers that would open all the doors she needed. She

*"Nothing attracts me like a closed door," said Bourke-White, center. She was the first foreign photographer allowed to record the Soviet Union's progress from an economy based on agriculture to one based on industry.*

later wrote that her documents carried "enough red stamps, purple seals, and red ink signatures to impress any Russian in any province."[9] Not only that, the Soviet government agreed to pay her expenses. It was proud of the country's progress toward industrialization and wanted the world to see it through her photographs.

With her interpreter, Lida Ivanovna, by her side, Bourke-White set out on her Soviet adventure. First she went to the city of Dnieprostroi, where she photographed the world's largest dam as it was being built on the Dnieper River by sixteen thousand workers. As usual, she charged in, climbing scaffolding and balancing herself and her cameras in moving cranes to get her shots.

Next Bourke-White traveled to Rostov to photograph the modern collective farms that were being created there to increase agricultural productivity. From Rostov, she went on to Novorossisk, a seaport on the Black Sea, where she photographed the Soviet Union's oldest and largest cement factory. In her travels, she came to realize that the Soviet people idolized the machine just as she did.[10]

Bourke-White completed her tour in Stalingrad, photographing a steel plant, as well as the *tractorstroi,* or tractor factory. She discovered the Soviets' special reverence for the tractor as a symbol of their progress in agriculture.

Once her trip was complete, Bourke-White returned to Moscow and prepared for her journey home. In just five weeks she had covered five thousand miles and had taken eight hundred photographs. But before she could leave, Soviet censors, or inspectors, had to review each of her photographs. For them to do that, she had to develop all eight hundred negatives.

The tremendous task kept her busy—and without sleep—for the next thirty-six hours. The first afternoon and night, she and her two assistants bathed all the negatives in the developing solution. She described the grueling process in her autobiography: "All the next day I spent on my knees in front of the bathtub. I did not stop to eat. I did not even remove my hands from the tub. My friends fed me sandwiches while I worked all day with my arms in cold water up to my elbows."[11]

Then she had to find a way to dry all eight hundred pictures. Her solution was to string a maze of cord from her hotel room ceiling, pinning each dripping photograph to the cord like clothes on a clothesline. Finally, she was finished: "Exhausted and triumphant, I threw myself on the bed, and, under the gentle rain of films dripping from the ceiling, I at once fell asleep."[12]

Once her photos had been inspected and passed by the Soviet censors, Bourke-White was permitted to board a train that would return her to Berlin. Back in the United States, Bourke-White published forty of her Soviet photographs and wrote about her experiences in a book called *Eyes on Russia.* She dedicated the book to her father. *Eyes on Russia* received favorable reviews, and her photographs were highly praised.[13]

Bourke-White's book and photographs about the Soviet Union increased her fame. Americans were fascinated with this huge country. Bourke-White's photos and her book helped answer many of their questions. By the early 1930s, she was one of the best-known photographers in America.[14] She also began giving lectures about her experiences and impressions of the Soviet Union.

For each of the following two summers, the Soviet government invited Bourke-White back to continue her photographic record of the country's progress. On her third trip, she spent most of her time in the country-side rather than in the industrial centers. She traveled by horseback in the Caucasus Mountains, accompanied by several local government officials. Their journey was rugged, going into areas foreigners had rarely visited. If they needed food, they simply stopped in a village, slaughtered a sheep, and roasted it over an open fire. At night they slept in mountain caves.

The villagers they encountered had never seen an "Amerikanka" before, and they were eager to offer hospitality. Bourke-White and her escorts spent many evenings with local peasants who entertained them with festive singing, folk dancing, drinking, and toasts.

The experience was a perfect opportunity for Bourke-White to see the people of the Soviet Union close-up, and to photograph them for the rest of the world. She made the most of the opportunity.

# Shifting Focus

By 1934, America had been suffering from the Great Depression for almost five years. Millions of people were without jobs; the future looked grim. The Depression's length and severity would make it the worst economic disaster in the history of the industrial world.

Along with the country's change of circumstances, many people's interests were shifting as well. Moving away from the confident and self-centered attitudes of the 1920s, a rising interest and concern about the lives of everyday Americans began to grow. Because of the country's economic suffering, more and more people wanted to know about their fellow citizens. How were they coping in the depressed economy?[1]

A new kind of journalism, called documentary literature, was emerging.[2] Newspapers and magazines began printing articles about ordinary people and their lives. Along with facts, these features usually carried a strong emotional message as they exposed the day-to-day hardships that many people faced. With words and photos, documentary literature gave Americans a greater understanding of what was going on in their country.

*Fortune* followed the trend toward documentary literature. Over time, fewer and fewer of its articles featured American industry and the business world.[3] Instead, the magazine began concentrating on stories about people and their lives.

Bourke-White was changing as well. Since her second trip to the Soviet Union, her attention and focus had been shifting.[4] Rather than being exclusively interested in machines and industry, she had begun to notice the faces behind the machines. As her work with *Fortune* continued, her interest in people and their problems deepened, changing the content and style of her photographs.

In the summer of 1934, *Fortune* sent Bourke-White to photograph a story on the Great Plains. Since 1930, a severe drought had devastated the plains. With no rain, much of the farmland had turned to dust. No longer able to support vegetation, the dust simply blew away. Known as the Dust Bowl, the region was a wasteland of dying livestock and suffering farmers and their families.

Chartering a tiny two-seater plane and heading

west, Bourke-White soon discovered the magnitude of the Dust Bowl disaster. It stretched north into the Dakotas and as far south as Texas. Later, in an article, she wrote, "This year there is an atmosphere of utter hopelessness. Nothing to do. No use digging out your chicken coops and pigpens after the last duster because the next one will be coming along soon. No use trying to keep the house clean. No use fighting off that foreclosure any longer. No use even hoping to give your cattle anything to chew on when their food crops have literally blown out of the ground."[5]

Bourke-White's experience photographing the Dust Bowl sharpened her career focus. She would concentrate on social and economic injustice. She knew the power of photographs to influence people's thinking.[6]

As her social awareness deepened, Bourke-White faced an internal struggle. As a part-time photographer for *Fortune,* she had spent the other half of her time working for advertising clients, photographing products such as cars, tires, food, and cosmetics. These clients paid her top dollar to make their products look good in magazine ads. But Bourke-White was becoming increasingly dissatisfied with that kind of work. Advertising often involved making a product look better than it really was. She said, "There is a conflict, and it has been bothering me more and more. I have come to see that, to make a successful advertising picture, I must see things through the advertiser's eyes. And that means something different from seeing things through the eyes of the artist, particularly if the artist has some social conceptions."[7]

Eventually, she made a decision. She would refuse to take any more advertising work that she could not do in a creative and constructive way.[8] She soon turned down an offer to create advertising photographs that would pay $1,000 each—her highest offer ever. By the end of 1936, she had stopped all her advertising work. Instead she used her photographs to convey the meaning of the times.[9]

In 1936, Bourke-White was ready to work on another book project. This time she wanted to educate Americans about the social conditions in their

Drought Erosion, *South Dakota, 1934. After photographing the wasteland of the Dust Bowl and seeing the suffering of the farmers, Bourke-White changed the focus of her career. "Suddenly it was the people who counted," she said.*

country. Instead of doing the writing herself, as she had with *Eyes on Russia,* she hoped to work with an experienced writer who had a similar interest. A chance would soon present itself.

Erskine Caldwell, a prominent American author, was interested in writing a documentary book about the desperate living conditions of the 10 million sharecroppers and tenant farmers in the South. A novelist and short story writer, Caldwell had come to fame through his best-selling books *Tobacco Road* and *God's Little Acre.* He wrote about the poor people of rural America. But many of Caldwell's readers did not believe his books portrayed life in the South accurately. Caldwell wanted to prove *Tobacco Road* true, along with the racism and poverty it revealed.[10] For his project he would need an expert photographer. It was just the sort of opportunity Bourke-White was looking for.

At first, the project seemed perfect for both. But their plans soon hit obstacles. Bourke-White needed to postpone the project; Caldwell grew weary of her delays. Once they began work, they found their styles clashed. Bourke-White was temperamental and emotional. She often cried if she did not get her way. Caldwell was reserved. As he wrote to his wife, "The trouble is Bourke-White is in the habit of getting her own way—and so am I—what happens when we fall out is all that can be imagined."[11]

Before long, their tempers reached the boiling point. Caldwell was ready to call the project off. On the evening he went to her hotel room to get the matter settled, Bourke-White once again persuaded him to continue the project. That night, the couple also began a love affair that would last for the next six years.

The next morning they began developing a working style that suited them both. They drove through the back roads of the Deep South, looking for subjects to photograph. Caldwell would stop the car, amble up to the person, and start a conversation. Meanwhile, Bourke-White would set up her camera equipment. Most of the people they encountered were shy of strangers or fearful that they might be made fun of.[12] But Caldwell was a native southerner, and his easygoing style and southern drawl helped set the farmers and their families at ease.

Once Caldwell got permission to photograph, Bourke-White took over like a movie director. She wrote,

> *Sometimes I would set up the camera in a corner of the room, sit some distance away from it with a remote control in my hand, and watch our people while Mr. Caldwell talked with them. It might be an hour before their faces or gestures gave us what we were trying to express, but the instant it occurred the scene was imprisoned on a sheet of film before they knew what had happened.*[13]

Together, Caldwell and Bourke-White completed their book, called *You Have Seen Their Faces.* Caldwell's words and Bourke-White's sixty-four black-and-white photographs captured the poverty of

*In* You Have Seen Their Faces, *Bourke-White's photographs captured the poverty of the Deep South. This little boy in East Feliciana Parish, Louisiana, described his dog Blackie as "good for nothing, he's just an old hound dog."*

the rural South. Caldwell described the bleak future of the tenant farmer:

> *There was a time when heads were put together in an effort to devise ways and means of making two blades of grass grow where only one had grown before. Now heads are being beaten against the ground in a desperate struggle to keep the one blade alive. Hopes of having two bales of cotton in place of one, of having two dollars instead of one dollar, have given way to hopes of being able to make half a bale of cotton, to make fifty cents.*[14]

Bourke-White caught a range of emotions in the faces she photographed: hopelessness, resignation, desperation, anger, acceptance. She showed whites and blacks, young and old, barefoot women cooking at open fires, people of all ages unkempt, uncombed, and needing care. Worry and despair could be seen in the deeply lined, sunbaked faces. Other photos revealed the farmers' flimsy shacks, with no electricity or plumbing, and old newspapers plastered to the walls to provide insulation. This was a world where people slept on dirt floors, knew a steady diet of cornbread and molasses, and had no hope for better days ahead.

Caldwell and Bourke-White hoped to give their readers a true picture of life in a part of America.[15] And they succeeded. *You Have Seen Their Faces* became a landmark book in documentary literature. It received enthusiastic critical acclaim and sold well.[16]

# A Passion
# for Pictures

On November 23, 1936, a new magazine was launched in America. It would become legendary for its quality, its spectacular photographs, and its illuminating portrayal of life in the United States and throughout the world. That magazine, *Life,* was another of Henry Luce's publishing creations.

Unlike *Fortune,* which was geared primarily to American business, *Life* was aimed at the general public. Luce thought people were hungry for a magazine that would tell them more about the world they lived in. And he knew they wanted to receive that information in a format that included lots of pictures.[1]

Not surprisingly, Luce wanted Bourke-White to shift her work from *Fortune* to *Life.* She was delighted.

She wrote, "The idea of [*Life*] is to present the news of the world in pictures. It is the kind of work I most enjoy doing."[2]

She agreed to work for *Life* ten months each year, saving only two months for other projects. *Life* also hired three other top photographers of the day: Alfred Eisenstadt, Tom McAvoy, and Peter Stackpole. The support staff for Bourke-White included Oscar Graubner, her highly talented darkroom technician who would become head of *Life*'s photo lab. *Life* also hired Peggy Sargent, Bourke-White's trusted secretary, along with two additional assistants.

For her first *Life* assignment, Luce sent Bourke-White to the little frontier town of New Deal, Montana. The town had sprung up around the construction of the nearby Fort Peck Dam. The dam was one of thousands of projects initiated by President Franklin D. Roosevelt in an effort to create more jobs in the country. The Fort Peck Dam would be the world's largest earth-filled dam.

When the editors at *Life* saw Bourke-White's photographs from New Deal, they decided to use them as *Life*'s first cover and lead story.[3] Not only had she captured powerful pictures of the dam itself, she also went behind the scenes to photograph the little town. Her photos showed the roughness and simplicity of life there. She shot a dance hall where young women danced with the lonely dam workers for a dime. She shot photos of the primitive wooden shacks where the townspeople lived. Tired workers at the end of a long day drinking whiskey and beer at the Bar X saloon

*Bourke-White's picture of Fort Peck Dam in Montana appeared on the cover of the first issue of* Life *magazine.*

were the subjects of yet another photo. She even got a shot of the barmaid's four-year-old daughter playing on top of the bar, as she did each evening.

*Life*'s first cover story showed the building of a major dam as part of America's hope for recovery from the Great Depression. It also told a human interest story—depicting the lives of individual Americans as they built a future. *Life*'s staff had expected the powerful construction pictures Bourke-White was famous for. What she gave them, however, was much more. The magazine's introduction described the story as "a human document of American frontier life."[4] Bourke-White set a standard for excellence that would establish the tone for the magazine's future.[5]

From its very first issue, *Life* was an overwhelming success. Published weekly, copies sold out in hours. During the first month, dealers across the country begged to increase their orders by as much as 500 percent.

One of the magazine's goals was to show American life in all its variety. An ad for the magazine claimed, "One of *Life*'s functions is introducing the Vermonter and the Californian to each other. . . . Thus *Life* serves as a force for creating understanding between widely separated, variously occupied people."[6] The magazine wanted to pull the country together, building readers' knowledge about—and love for—America.

*Life*'s tone was consistently upbeat. Publisher Henry Luce said, "*Life* has a bias. (Life is in favor of the human race, and it is hopeful. *Life* likes life.)"[7] And the magazine's readership responded. By the end of its first year, *Life* had built a circulation of 1.5 million readers.

With *Life*'s success, Bourke-White's fame grew as well. Her photographs were now seen regularly by millions. With the magazine she continued her hectic pace, covering stories throughout the country. In 1937, when the Ohio River overflowed in one of the worst floods in American history, *Life* sent Bourke-White to capture the story. With three-fourths of the city under water, she was forced to travel through the streets by raft.

Another time she was in Washington, D.C., for a story on the Supreme Court. To get the photo she wanted of the Capitol, she set up her equipment in the middle of Washington's busiest street, halting streetcars and jamming traffic for blocks.

She also did a story about everyday life in Muncie, Indiana. Another *Life* photo essay showed the paper manufacturing industry. She even did an investigative piece about the tyrannical rule of Mayor Hague in Jersey City, New Jersey. After she photographed the city's sweatshops—in which children worked for pennies an hour—the mayor became so angry that he had her arrested and her cameras smashed. Bourke-White was prepared, though. She had already sent her film ahead to the *Life* offices.

For some of her stories, Bourke-White added to the drama of her photos by getting shots from airplanes. These contributed to her reputation as a daredevil. First, she would have one of the plane's doors removed. Then she would tie herself to a seat with a rope. That way, she could lean way out of the doorway with her twenty-pound camera to take shots of the scenes she wanted far below.

Despite her fame and experience, Bourke-White did not grow sloppy with her work. She was still as much of a perfectionist as ever. She treated each assignment as if it were her most important. In an interview she explained, "Some of my best pictures represent five hundred films destroyed [used]. . . . But to me the result was all that counted."[8]

During this time, Bourke-White and Erskine Caldwell saw each other whenever they could squeeze in visits between Bourke-White's travels for *Life*. But while they were devoted to each other, each was torn by conflicting issues. Caldwell was tormented by indecision between his love for Bourke-White and his love for his wife, Helen. They had three young children together, and his family weighed heavily on his conscience and his heart.[9]

Bourke-White's concern was that marriage to Caldwell would interfere with her independence and her work. Her career was her first love. She was afraid that marriage would tie her down in ways she would come to resent.[10] And despite his gentleness and devotion to her, there were also Caldwell's dark moods to contend with. They struck without warning and brought long periods of silence. Often he shut her out for hours or even days and then erupted in a violent rage of temper.[11] The couple continued their relationship, neither completely comfortable with the situation, yet not knowing what to do.

In July 1937, *Life* sent Bourke-White to the Arctic. She was to accompany Sir John Buchan Tweedsmuir, the new governor-general of Canada, as he toured the remote areas of the country. Traveling on an ancient, wood-burning steamboat, Bourke-White and Tweedsmuir visited tiny towns along their way. At each stop, they delivered mail, groceries, and supplies. Before she was through with the assignment, she would travel thousands of miles across the Arctic tundra.

Having never lost her fascination with insects and their life cycles, Bourke-White took butterfly chrysalises with her on the trip. In between photos, she guarded the chrysalises, eating her meals on deck so she would not miss their progress. Before the trip was over, ten newborn mourning cloak butterflies were released into their new home.

When that assignment was completed, *Life* asked Bourke-White to charter a plane and photograph the Arctic Ocean in the summer. She found a pilot to take her in an old Ford seaplane. An Episcopal bishop joined them on his way to minister to the Inuit in remote villages. Along the way, Bourke-White got the shots she wanted. But near-disaster hit when a blinding fog descended on the plane. All landmarks quickly disappeared and the pilot was unable to fly. Finally they were able to land on a tiny, rocky island. They settled in, hoping the fog would lift. To pass the time and keep their spirits up, the little group brewed tea, sang songs, and played games.

At the end of the second day, the fog showed signs of lifting. They quickly herded back into the plane and made it through a fierce rainstorm to a tiny Inuit settlement. From there they were able to refuel the plane and return to civilization and safety.

Back in New York, Bourke-White continued with her work. In the spring of 1938, *Life* sent her to Czechoslovakia. By this time, war clouds were darkening over Europe as Hitler's Germany continued to build up military strength. The world was watching and waiting to see what would happen next. *Life* wanted Bourke-White to bring back the story in pictures.

Caldwell, now divorced from his wife, accompanied Bourke-White on the trip. They hoped to use their research to create another book together. They stayed in Czechoslovakia for five months, photographing and writing, talking with the people, and exploring the countryside. Returning home in August, they put together their book, *North of the Danube*. It was published in April 1939 to good reviews. Once again, Bourke-White had been in the right place at the right time. Americans everywhere were eager for information and photographs about Eastern Europe as German troops massed along Czechoslovakia's borders, threatening invasion.

Soon after their return to the United States, Caldwell and Bourke-White bought a house in Darien, Connecticut. Located fifty miles north of New York City, the white, two-story clapboard home sat atop a wooded hill. They thought it was an ideal place to continue their work together.

Early in 1939, Bourke-White at last agreed to marry Caldwell. She continued to have doubts but

*The writer and the photographer: Erskine Caldwell and Margaret Bourke-White worked together on projects all around the world.*

could not bring herself to leave him.[12] She hoped that if they were married, the frequent strains between them would be resolved.

The couple flew to Reno, Nevada, where they could get a marriage license without the waiting period imposed by other states. On the way, Bourke-White wrote a marriage contract of rules for the newlyweds to live by. With his signature, Caldwell agreed to her terms. They would work out any conflict by midnight of the day it had started, he would try to control his moods, he would be courteous to her friends, and he would give her the freedom she needed for her work.

With marriage license in hand, along with a minister who agreed to accompany them, they drove to Silver City, an abandoned mining town near Reno. As the sun set on the desert sands, Bourke-White and Caldwell were married on February 27, 1939, in a dusty old church, with their taxi driver as a witness.

Several months later, in October 1939, Bourke-White was sent to Europe to photograph the war for *Life*. Bourke-White's photograph of Winston Churchill, who became the British prime minister, was published on the cover of the magazine, but *Life* did not publish most of the other pictures she took.

By March 1940 Bourke-White's enchantment with her work for *Life* had diminished. She felt that her photos were not featured in the magazine often enough and that she was not getting enough credit for her work.

When Ralph Ingersoll, a former managing editor

for *Life,* approached Bourke-White about working on a daily newspaper he wanted to start, she was interested. Ingersoll's *PM* would be the first photographic newspaper in history. He planned to devote more than half of each issue to pictures. Its focus would be on social issues and injustice in the nation. Ingersoll enticed Bourke-White with promises that she would travel less for *PM* than she was doing for *Life.* He also thought she and Caldwell could work on stories together for the newspaper.

Bourke-White resigned from *Life* and went to work for *PM.* Her decision was a triumph for *PM.* Hiring Bourke-White added prestige and credibility to the newspaper from the start.

But the new partnership would not last. The newspaper's stories didn't have the scope and depth that Bourke-White's photos required. And working for a daily meant she did not have the time she needed to get the high-quality pictures she demanded of herself. In October, after only six months with *PM,* Bourke-White asked to return to *Life.*

*Life* put her back on the road immediately. This time her assignment was to travel across the country and do a story on America. What were Americans thinking? What was the mood of the country? What did Americans think about the war in Europe? *Life* thought its readers wanted to know.

Caldwell joined her on this extended trip and they began traveling west. Their friends received their Christmas card that year with a picture of the couple perched atop a freight train, with typewriter and camera poised for action. By the time their trip was over, they had zigzagged ten thousand miles from coast to coast.

Although *Life* never used their material, Bourke-White and Caldwell put it to good use, creating their third book together, *Say, Is This the USA?* Published in 1941, it was their least successful book, having no human conflict as its focus.[13]

# Dodging Bombs

On March 20, 1941, Bourke-White headed to the Soviet Union once again. This time her trip would put her in the center of a war zone. Flying from Los Angeles to Hong Kong with Caldwell by her side, their plane dodged Japanese warplanes on the way. When they arrived in Hong Kong, the Soviet ambassador to Hong Kong told her to return to the United States. The western borders of the Soviet Union were closed to travelers because of the increasing threat of war. They could be captured by enemy troops and held as prisoners of war.

That only doubled Bourke-White's resolve to get into the Soviet Union. So they pushed on to Chungking, the provisional capital of China, where they were able to get Soviet visas, despite the danger. From there they traveled on to Moscow, finally reaching the city after more than a month of travel and delays.

In the Soviet Union, she and Caldwell began a trip that took them to the wheat fields of the Ukraine and to factories in several Soviet cities. Her job was to photograph the country's progress since her trip there a decade earlier. They ended their tour at the Black Sea for a few days of vacation.

But the couple's plans were quickly interrupted. By this time most of Europe had been conquered by the Germans. Now Hitler turned his sights on the Soviet Union. On June 22, 1941, the Germans staged a massive attack against the Soviets. With that, they broke the nonaggression pact they had signed with Josef Stalin two years earlier.

Caldwell and Bourke-White caught the first train back to Moscow. There, the United States ambassador ordered every United States citizen out of the country. With war breaking out, he could not ensure their safety. *Life* was worried about Bourke-White, too. But Bourke-White refused to leave. She was indignant at the very thought of leaving. She wrote, "Surely . . . anybody would know that I would start throwing my lenses like hand grenades at anyone who tried to carry me away from such a scoop as this."[1] Later, the ambassador relented, and she and Caldwell were allowed to stay.

The next problem was a wartime restriction on photography in the country. Official orders stated that anyone caught with a camera would be shot on sight. Margaret pleaded for special permission to take photos. She was now the only Western photographer in the country. She had sole access to the biggest story of the day. It was a photojournalist's dream.

She and Caldwell moved into Moscow's magnificent National Hotel. They had a suite of richly furnished rooms, complete with crystal chandeliers, a grand piano, and a pale blue ceiling painted with pink and white cupids. Best of all, their balcony looked directly out onto the Kremlin (government headquarters), Lenin's Tomb, and Red Square.

On July 19, Germany dropped its first bombs on the blacked-out city. Residents, including Bourke-White and Caldwell, were herded into a massive underground subway shelter where they had to remain through the night. After five and a half hours in the shelter, Bourke-White was wild with frustration. She and her camera were missing out on the action aboveground.[2]

The next night, when the bombs began falling, Bourke-White took her cameras and headed to the U.S. embassy. From the building's roof, she began photographing the spectacle. As she turned to go back inside the building, a bomb hit just fifty yards away, knocking her flat and showering her with broken glass from nearby windows. She barely missed being crushed by a heavy air compressor that landed inches from her head.

From that night on, she and Caldwell decided to stay in their hotel room during the bombing raids.

Each evening around midnight, the air-raid sirens signaled to everyone to go underground. But Bourke-White did not rush to the bomb shelter. Instead she threw herself under the big bed in their suite. Caldwell would hide behind a sofa under a white bearskin rug. When the inspection wardens came by to make sure everyone had evacuated, they would see no one in the couple's suite.

Then Bourke-White set up her cameras to begin photographing from the balcony. As protection, she wore a Soviet helmet so heavy, she said, "I had to develop a whole new set of neck muscles."[3] With the Germans often concentrating their bombs on the Kremlin, she had a perfect view. She wrote, "The opening air raids over Moscow possessed a magnificence that I have never seen matched in any other man-made spectacle. It was as though the German pilots and the Russian anti-aircraft gunners had been handed enormous brushes dipped in radium paint and were executing abstract designs with the sky as their vast canvas."[4]

Bourke-White also received special permission for a private session to photograph the Soviet leader, Josef Stalin. Throughout the city, gigantic marble statues of Stalin towered high above the crowds. Since coming to Moscow, Bourke-White had been curious about this fierce man. Indeed, Stalin would prove to be a difficult subject. After waiting for two hours, she was finally ushered into his Kremlin office for the shoot. Stalin was known for his power and ruthlessness. How would she ever get a portrait that would show the man beneath this icy exterior? Finally, just by accident, her flashbulbs spilled from her pocket across the floor. For an instant Stalin broke his stony glare and laughed. Later she described the moment. "When his face lighted up with a smile, the change was miraculous. It was as though a second personality had come to the front, genial, cordial, and kindly."[5] With her camera, Bourke-White was able to capture the hint of a smile in his eyes before his face hardened again.

Just before leaving Moscow, Bourke-White and Caldwell were given permission to go with a small group of war correspondents to the Soviet front near Smolensk. Enduring primitive conditions and frequent rain, they slept on the floors of abandoned cottages or in tents and ate whatever they could find—raw fish, goose, black bread, and cheese.

During the trip Bourke-White wore her red coat inside out so she would not be as likely to attract enemy gunfire. The roofs of their cars were covered with cut greenery in an attempt at camouflage, reminding her of "a nursery on wheels."[6] While on that trip, she got photos of enemy planes as they flew low overhead, and villages just after they had been hit by German bombs.

Back in the United States, Bourke-White began a book about her experiences, called *Shooting the Russian War*. It would be published in 1942. This time, rather than combining talents with her husband, Bourke-White created the book entirely on her own, writing the text that accompanied the photos.

The book was well received by the public and got good critical reviews.

The United States had entered World War II in December 1941. By the spring of 1942, Bourke-White wanted to return to the war front. Her husband was furious. How could she leave him again and go into such danger? Yet he knew she could not stand to be at home missing all the action overseas. He also knew their marriage was falling apart.[7]

With *Life*'s help, Bourke-White became the first woman photographer accredited to the United States Army Air Force. That meant she had the army's permission to take war photographs. Before she left, the air force had a uniform specially designed for her. Wearing a military uniform would immediately identify her as part of the U.S. armed forces. A uniform would also help her blend in with the soldiers to prevent her from becoming an obvious enemy target.

Early in August she was off to England to photograph the first B-17 bombers the United States had sent there. While in England, Bourke-White received a cable from Caldwell that would change her life. After all their ups and downs, he wanted a divorce. With a series of overseas telegrams, the decision was made. As she had done when her marriage to Chapman ended years before, Bourke-White chose to take the best from the relationship and leave the rest behind. She wrote, "We had five good, productive years—with occasional tempests, it's true, but with some real happiness. I was relieved when it was all over and

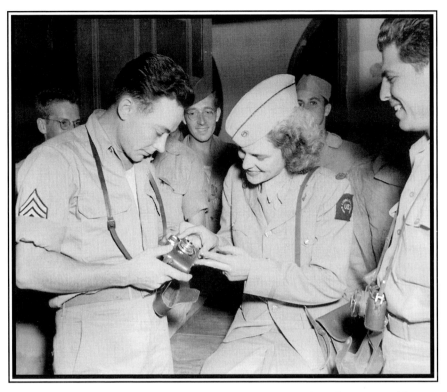

*Bourke-White wore a military uniform to blend in during World War II. "War correspondents see a great deal of the world," she said. "Our obligation is to pass it on to others."*

glad we parted with a mutual affection and respect which still endures."[8]

In England Bourke-White began hearing rumors that the Allied forces were planning to invade North Africa. She knew this would be a huge story. Desperate to be in the action, she got permission to transfer there.

But army officials were worried for her safety. They refused to let her fly to North Africa. Instead, she would go by ship convoy. In a twist of fate, her ship was torpedoed, and it sank.

Once rescued and deposited safely in North Africa, Bourke-White became the first woman to be given permission to take photographs during a bombing mission. It had long been a goal for her, and on January 22, 1943, she got her wish. The target was the Tunis airfield. It was an important transportation hub for the Germans, who had captured it from the French. The Allies wanted it destroyed.

Heading out that morning, Bourke-White was in the lead plane of a group of thirty-three bombers. She wore a heavy, fleece-lined leather jumpsuit and electric mittens to combat the temperature of forty degrees below zero that she would face when the plane reached its cruising altitude of twenty-one thousand feet.

Was she scared? Yes. But fear was not about to stop her. She wrote, "You know you may not come back; but that is one of the hazards of the road you have chosen, so you thrust that thought as far into the back of your head as possible."[9]

All during the flight Bourke-White was either snapping pictures as fast as her camera would allow or taking notes. As the bombers approached the airfield, she could see people on the ground running in fear and trucks speeding to shelter.

After her plane dropped its bombs, it immediately turned, weaving and changing altitude to avoid gunfire from the ground. Behind them an inferno of flames erupted on the ground as ninety tons of bombs hit their target.

Soon her pilot realized they were being pursued by German fighters. One got as close as twenty yards from them before it was shot down. Bourke-White's plane was hit twice in the wing, receiving minor damage. The plane made it back to the base safely. Two other planes in their group were not so lucky. Yet the mission was a success. Bourke-White had gotten her photographs, and the bombers had destroyed forty German planes and damaged forty more.

By September 1943, Bourke-White once again ventured into danger. This time she wanted to see the war from the ground. To do that, she obtained permission to photograph the Services of Supply branch of the army. These were the people who supplied the troops with food, supplies, ammunition, and medical services. Her job was to record their vital, behind-the-scenes mission.

To get the story, Bourke-White spent five months with the Fifth Army as it fought in Italy. The Allied troops were moving slowly north to retake the country from the Germans. They had reached the Cassino Valley, where the surrounding mountains sheltered many German troops. This gave the Germans clear shots at any Allied soldiers in the valley below. The Allies suffered so many casualties there that the soldiers nicknamed it "Purple Heart Valley."

Bourke-White stayed with the soldiers as they fought for the valley. One of her jobs was to photograph the engineers risking their lives to rebuild bridges and roads the Germans had bombed. Bourke-White usually shot from a tripod, to steady her camera during artillery fire.

For part of the time she stayed in a fourteenth-century monastery, along with the monks who lived there. But out in the field, she often slept in foxholes, despite the constant rain. She ate army rations of powdered eggs and chipped beef right along with the soldiers. She learned to jump from her jeep and into a ditch when enemy shells came her way.

Bourke-White found the shelling to be particularly frightening. Her fear caught her by surprise. After all, she had endured enemy bombings in Moscow, China, and England. But shelling from artillery guns on the ground was different. She later explained that with shelling, the enemy was after a specific target. If you were unlucky enough to be at that target, from your point of view he was after you. "[It] was intensely and horribly personal."[10]

She had to be especially careful of land mines. The Germans had sprinkled these explosives throughout the territory. Whenever she stepped off the road, she had to be careful to step only inside existing boot prints or jeep tire tracks to avoid being blown up by a mine.

Bourke-White's work in Italy took all the courage she could muster. Leaving the front each day, she was overcome with a sense of relief as well as guilt. Later she wrote about her feelings: "I find it difficult to express the blessed relief, the quickening joy, with which you find yourself heading home from the front.

Each mile in the road brings a lightening of the heart."[11]

Bourke-White took aerial shots of the pockmarked Cassino Valley several times from a two-seater Piper Cub airplane. That became yet another dangerous adventure. The Piper Cub was used to spot enemy guns, but it carried no weapons. The plane's only defense was its ability to fly low and fast.

Once, while Bourke-White was taking photographs from the Piper Cub, the plane was spotted and followed by four German fighters ready to shoot it out of the sky. Instantly, her pilot dove so deeply she found herself almost standing on her head. They barely made it back to safety, and only by flying low, too close to the treetops for the fighters to follow.

*"You know you may not come back; but that is one of the hazards of the road you have chosen," wrote Bourke-White. Here, on the battlefield in Italy in 1943, she insisted on being in the middle of the action.*

Bourke-White also photographed the Eleventh Field Hospital. The hospital was set up near a ridge of hills bordering the valley, very close to the frontlines of battle.

Bourke-White spent an entire night photographing the surgeons at work. Shells screamed in two-way traffic over their heads throughout the night. Despite the danger, the doctors and nurses continued their work, using only flashlights to illuminate what they were doing. Each time an enemy shell was heard from overhead, they all had to stop and drop to the floor to prepare for the hit. Once the danger was over, they went back to work—checking the plasma bottles and transfusion needles of the men on the operating tables, changing rubber gloves, sterilizing instruments, and picking up operations that had been interrupted. All the while, Bourke-White shot her photos.

The anguish of the patients, along with the bravery of the medical personnel, tugged at Bourke-White's heart. She wrote, "I realized that people at home wanted to know what their boys were going through. They had a right to know, and it was my assignment to portray the reality of war as I found it."[12]

When she returned to the United States she discovered to her horror that *Life* had never received her package of hospital photos. Somehow, they had been lost at the Pentagon. She was wild with dismay and fury.[13] She even went to the Pentagon to look through shelves and drawers, searching for her lost treasure of photos. They were never discovered, and she never got over her bitterness at their loss.

Back at home, Bourke-White wrote her next book. Increasingly, she found the need to express herself in writing, as well as in photographs. She wrote, "Much as I love cameras, they can't do everything."[14] In *They Called It "Purple Heart Valley,"* she wrote about her experiences at the Italian front. The book was very popular and was reprinted five times.

Bourke-White's final experience in World War II came as the war was drawing to a close. She joined General George S. Patton's Third Army as it traveled east through Germany on the way to Berlin, the capital of Hitler's Third Reich.

On April 11, 1945, Patton's troops approached Buchenwald, a concentration camp near Weimar, Germany. They were aware that the camp was nearby. Press reports had leaked stories of the Nazi concentration camps throughout the war, yet few knew the full extent of the camps' horrors. Buchenwald would become the first German concentration camp to be liberated by the Allies.

That morning began quietly for Buchenwald's 21,400 inmates. They had known of the army's progress for days. Low-flying American Spitfire bombers and scout planes had been seen overhead in increasing numbers. The prison camp officers had been frantically destroying their official records.[15] The muffled sound of artillery fire—first distant, then closer each day—confirmed the secret radio broadcasts and press reports of the approaching Allies.

Just after 4:00 P.M., the first American scout car arrived at Buchenwald's gates. Miles of barbed wire fence stretched in both directions from the reddish-brown wooden pavilion. Behind the wire stood a series of long, low barracks. As Bourke-White approached the camp, Patton's military police were rounding up Weimar's citizens so they could witness the camp's liberation. The stench of death, disease, and despair hung heavily in the air.

An eyewitness later reported, "The inmates liberated by our forces were skeletons . . . many of the captives [had been] professional soldiers . . . and they pulled their wasted bodies into gallant salutes as Eisenhower, Patton, and their staffs passed them."[16] No German guards or commanders remained. They had all fled into the surrounding woods two hours earlier.

Despite all Bourke-White had experienced so far in the war, she was not prepared for the sight she met when she reached Buchenwald. Stunned but determined, she began to photograph the camp's living and dead.

Inside the gate was a spacious courtyard made of rough flagstones. There she recorded on film a pile of corpses stacked high. With only the thinnest covering of skin, mouths gaping, legs and arms askew, these prisoners' remains revealed the terror, indignity, and suffering they had endured.[17]

Framing her shots through the barbed wire, Bourke-White also photographed some of Buchenwald's survivors in their gray-and-white striped uniforms and ragged hats and jackets.[18] They stared blankly as her camera flashed. Her photographs captured the atrocities of the concentration camp for the world to see.

With Bourke-White's pictures, Americans were forced to confront the truth of the Nazi atrocities for the first time. Remarking about her work as a war correspondent during World War II, Bourke-White later said, "We see a great deal of the world. Our obligation is to pass it on to others."[19] And pass it on, she did.

After her final series of World War II photographs, Bourke-White pulled her thoughts, impressions, and stories into yet another book, *Dear Fatherland, Rest Quietly,* published in 1946.

# 10

# The Toughest
# Challenge

$B$y the time World War II was
over, the United States was recognized as a major world
power. *Life* was the country's most popular magazine,
and Luce wanted that world view reflected in it. As
for Bourke-White, she continued as *Life*'s top
photographer. Her adventures were far from over.

In March 1946, *Life* sent Bourke-White to India.
The editors wanted her to photograph Mahatma
(Great Soul) Gandhi and do a story about India's
culture and quest for independence from Great
Britain. Gandhi had been leading his countrymen
since 1919 in nonviolent resistance to their British
rulers. Now independence seemed close at hand.

In India, Bourke-White asked for permission to
photograph Gandhi. His chief secretary explained that
before she could do so, she would have to learn to spin

thread on an old spinning wheel. To Gandhi, the wheel was a symbol of India's resistance to Great Britain: Indians could spin their own cloth and had no need for factory-made goods from England.

After Bourke-White took the lesson and managed to spin some thread, Gandhi agreed to see her. But he would allow no artificial lighting in his room. How could Bourke-White possibly take his photograph with only shadows for light? Finally, she was granted the use of three flashbulbs—but no more. For Bourke-White, famous for taking hundreds of shots of a single subject, getting the perfect picture in only three tries would be quite a challenge. In fact, the first two flashbulbs failed her. On her third try, she succeeded. Her portrait of Gandhi captured his simplicity, his gentleness, and his strength. It is one of her most memorable works.

When Bourke-White came home from India in October, she began a book about her experiences. When she ran into problems, she realized she needed to go back to the country to study it in even greater depth.

Returning in September 1947, Bourke-White found India in the midst of a religious war between Muslims and Hindus. Bloody riots swept from city to city as the two groups fought for control of the country.

When independence from Great Britain was declared earlier that year, India had been divided into two states. Hindus would live in the state of India, and a separate state called Pakistan was carved out for the Muslims. With this division, 10 million people were ousted from their homes. Bourke-White was on the scene to record the transition for the world.

Through her camera's lens she was able to convey the refugees' suffering and misery. All roads between the two states were clogged with peasants. Along the way, many thousands died, and their fly-covered bodies were strewn along the roadsides. Many others were injured or violated by marauding bands of thieves and thugs.

By the beginning of 1948, Bourke-White was preparing to leave India. At that time, the seventy-eight-year-old Gandhi had begun a hunger fast to protest the unending violence between the two religious groups. He said he would not eat until the violence ended and peace was restored.

*Mahatma Gandhi at his spinning wheel, Poona, India, 1946. "I was filled with an emotion as close to awe as a photographer can come," Bourke-White said of her meeting with Gandhi.*

For seven days Gandhi continued to fast, getting weaker each day. As the spiritual leader for millions of Indians, his suffering and message brought them together. With Gandhi very close to death, the warring factions agreed to a cease-fire. Bourke-White wrote, "The entire country had been stirred to its foundations, and the people bent their will toward peace."[1]

Shortly after Gandhi's fast, Bourke-White held her final interview with him. She would be the last foreign journalist to see him alive. He was assassinated later that day on his way to evening prayers. Bourke-White remained in India to photograph Gandhi's funeral procession. His rose-covered body was carried five miles to the banks of the sacred Jumna River. One million grief-stricken followers lined the roadway. Bourke-White stood on top of a truck, with her camera, to record the flames from his funeral pyre.

Altogether Bourke-White spent almost two years in India, photographing and learning to understand the culture. When she returned home, she was able to complete her book about the country, called *Halfway to Freedom: A Report on the New India.* It was published in 1949.

Toward the end of 1949, *Life* sent Bourke-White abroad again. This time she was to pursue a story about racial injustice in the Union of South Africa. Whites were only a fourth of the population of South Africa, but they ruled the country. Their system of government, apartheid, kept the races completely separated.

As a journalist, Bourke-White felt compelled to compose an unbiased photographic essay about life in South Africa. Yet she hated apartheid and ached for the country's blacks and the lives they led. She learned that black men were herded from their families for up to eighteen months at a stretch to work in South Africa's white-owned diamond and gold mines. After working underground all day, the men were crammed into windowless, concrete barracks to sleep at night. Blacks were forbidden to learn skilled trades, and they could not travel from their homes without official permission. It was a situation that Bourke-White wanted *Life*'s readers to understand.

She would spend five months in South Africa getting the story. She began by photographing the white South Africans who ruled the country. She got shots of government officials, sporting events, and social gatherings. She also photographed the spectacular South African scenery. But her real mission was to capture the misery of the black people who lived there. Government officials were not eager for her to photograph the people they oppressed. She was unsure of how to go about getting the photos that would tell their story.

One day a black woman happened to recognize Bourke-White from a newspaper picture. The woman had become a fan of Bourke-White's after seeing her work in *You Have Seen Their Faces*. She knew that Bourke-White used her photographs to try to help oppressed people. So she stopped the photographer, and from that chance meeting Bourke-White got the entrance she needed into the black South African culture.

One evening she was invited to photograph a group of black gold miners dressed in traditional costumes and dancing a tribal dance. She chose two who stood out for their exceptional grace and dignity. Next she wanted to photograph the same men at their work.

With some difficulty, Bourke-White got permission to photograph the two miners in the mine. Slowly, she made the two-mile descent in a wire cage into the dank, airless depths of the earth. Once there, she hardly recognized the two dancers whose eyes had shone so brightly the previous evening.[2]

In her photograph, the miners' dark torsos, dripping with sweat from their work, fill the frame. A mixture of emotions—hopelessness, anger, frustration—seem to emanate from their eyes. The low rock ceiling almost touches their work helmets, showing how they are trapped beneath the earth.

Bourke-White left South Africa in mid-April 1950. She was enraged at the conditions she had seen and felt powerless to make things better.[3] After that trip, she wanted nothing to do with gold or diamonds.[4] She hoped her photos could somehow make a difference.[5]

The next summer, *Life* sent Bourke-White to Kansas for a story on the Strategic Air Command. While there, she became the first woman to fly in a B-47 bomber. Later that year, she experimented with a new aerial photography technique by taking her pictures while dangling from a helicopter. This photo session nearly cost Bourke-White her life. While she was getting shots of a practice naval rescue mission, her helicopter lost power and plunged into

Chesapeake Bay. Luckily, no one was killed, but her cameras were lost to the bottom of the bay.

In 1952, Bourke-White went to Korea to cover the civil war that had been under way for about two years. Communist-ruled North Korea had invaded South Korea. The United Nations had sent forces to help South Korea. The war had already been given a lot of coverage in *Life* by other photographers. Bourke-White wanted to show it from a different angle. Rather than photograph soldiers and battles, she wanted to do a story about the people of Korea and how they were coping in their war-torn country.

As part of that story, she studied the bands of young Communist guerrillas—roving soldiers—that fought behind the United Nations lines. She would spend nine months photographing the small groups as they hid in the countryside and made raids against the United Nations forces. For this assignment, Bourke-White carried a .45 pistol and a longer-range carbine rifle because of the danger. She came to understand their reasons for fighting and the anguish of families split apart by civil war.

The next year, a disturbing physical sensation began to plague Bourke-White. She felt a dull ache in her left leg and arm. She paid no attention; after all, she had never been seriously ill in her life. But as time progressed, so did her symptoms. She found she had less and less control of her legs and arms. Her hands began to stiffen, making it difficult to use her cameras.

Despite her growing disability, Bourke-White continued her work for *Life*. Her next assignment was a story about the life of Jesuit priests. As part of that project, she worked with Father John LaFarge and completed another book, *A Report on the American Jesuits*. It was published in 1956.

She also began writing her autobiography, which she would work on over the next seven years. It would be her final major project. In the meantime, her symptoms were diagnosed as Parkinson's disease. This

*On assignment for* Life *magazine in 1953, Bourke-White photographed Jesuit priests.*

crippling illness affects the nerves and muscles. Over time, its victims lose control of their fingers, hands, arms, and legs. Their bodies shake, and speech can be affected. No one is sure why the disease strikes or how fast it will progress. But one thing was certain: There was no cure.

Bourke-White faced her Parkinson's with courage. She resolved to fight it with everything she had.[6] Losing her independence and career was her greatest fear. She turned to exercise. Doctors told her it was the only hope of slowing the progress of the disease. She began walking four miles each day to strengthen her legs. She crushed paper into balls and wrung out wet towels to keep her hands and arm muscles limber. She jumped rope, lifted weights, played badminton, danced, and played jacks. In an article for *Life* about her disease, Bourke-White remarked, "Beginning in 1955, everything I did became an exercise."[7]

Still the Parkinson's progressed. By 1957, she completed what would be her last story for *Life.* She had become too incapacitated to operate her cameras. Despite her difficulties, Bourke-White refused to give up. In an article as late as 1960, she told her interviewer, "I intend to continue taking pictures, and I intend to continue writing books." She planned to go back to *Life* assignments once her autobiography was completed.[8] The magazine kept her name on its masthead until 1969, when she officially retired.

Bourke-White would fight Parkinson's for nineteen years. She agreed to two risky operations on her brain, which seemed to improve her condition for a while. In 1963 her autobiography, *Portrait of Myself,* was published. But by then, Bourke-White's physical condition had deteriorated further. Having difficulty with balance and walking, she was confined to a wheelchair, her hands almost useless and her ability to speak impaired. She died on August 27, 1971, at the age of sixty-seven.

Margaret Bourke-White's spectacular life was over, but her reputation for excellence and daring lives on. With her special combination of talent, energy, and determination, she became the world's leading woman photojournalist.[9] She pioneered the field of industrial photography. Her work with *Life* magazine set the standard of excellence for a new way of reporting—the photographic essay. Bourke-White fulfilled her childhood vision of doing the things women never did, becoming an inspiration to women throughout America by excelling in a man's field.[10]

As a backdrop to her accomplishments, Margaret Bourke-White's life was filled with adventure. By the end of her career she had traveled a million miles and had taken photographs in forty-five countries.[11] In doing so, she became a legend, not only for the quality of her work, but for her daring and painstaking efforts to achieve that quality. Her work includes some of the most important photographs of the twentieth century, and her influence on photography and photojournalism will endure for years to come.[12]

# Chronology

1904—Margaret Bourke-White is born June 14 in the Bronx in New York City.

1906—White family moves to Bound Brook, New Jersey.

1921—Margaret graduates from high school; begins classes at Teachers College, Columbia University, New York City.

1922—Works as camp counselor and photographer; begins classes at the University of Michigan, Ann Arbor; meets Everett Chapman.

1924—Marries Everett Chapman; moves to Lafayette, Indiana; begins classes at Purdue University.

1925—Moves to Cleveland, Ohio; enrolls at Case Western Reserve University.

1926—Separates from Chapman; moves to Ithaca, New York; enrolls at Cornell University.

1927—Graduates from Cornell University; moves to Cleveland, Ohio; opens first photography studio.

1928—Finalizes divorce from Chapman; takes photographs of operations of Otis Steel Company.

1929—Joins staff of *Fortune* magazine as associate editor.

1930—Moves to New York City; travels to Germany and the Soviet Union to photograph the rise of industry.

1931—First book, *Eyes on Russia,* is published.

1934—Photographs the Dust Bowl for *Fortune* magazine.

1936—Meets Erskine Caldwell; begins research for *You Have Seen Their Faces;* joins *Life* magazine staff; photographs the Fort Peck Dam and New Deal, Montana, for *Life*'s first cover story.

1937—*You Have Seen Their Faces* is published.

1938—Travels to Czechoslovakia and Hungary with Caldwell.

1939—*North of the Danube* is published; marries Caldwell.

1940—Leaves *Life* to work for daily newspaper, *PM.*

1941—*Say, Is This the USA?* is published; returns to *Life* magazine; travels to the Soviet Union.

1942—Separates from Caldwell; is accredited as first American woman war correspondent to the U.S. Army Air Force; *Shooting the Russian War* is published.

1943—Becomes first woman to fly on a bombing mission with U.S. Air Force; *They Called It "Purple Heart Valley"* is published.

1945—Photographs liberation of Buchenwald concentration camp.

1946—*Dear Fatherland, Rest Quietly* is published; photographs Gandhi in India for *Life.*

1948—Receives Honorary Doctorate of Letters from Rutgers University.

1949—*Halfway to Freedom* is published.

1950—Takes photographs in South Africa for *Life.*

1951—Receives Honorary Doctorate of Arts from the University of Michigan.

1952—Photographs the Korean War; beginning of Parkinson's disease.

1953—Photographs Jesuits for *Life;* collaborates on *A Report on the American Jesuits.*

1957—Last photo essay for *Life.*

1963—*Portrait of Myself* is published.

1969—Officially retires from *Life* magazine.

1971—Bourke-White dies on August 27 in Darien, Connecticut.

## Chapter Notes

### Chapter 1. A Sinking Ship

1. Margaret Bourke-White, "Women in Lifeboats," *Life,* February 22, 1943, p. 48.

2. Ibid.

3. Ibid.

4. Vicki Goldberg, *Margaret Bourke-White: A Biography* (New York: Harper & Row, Publishers, 1986), p. 258.

5. Ibid.

6. Bourke-White, "Women in Lifeboats," p. 48.

7. Margaret Bourke-White, *Portrait of Myself* (New York: Simon & Schuster, 1963), p. 210.

8. Bourke-White, "Women in Lifeboats," pp. 48–49.

9. Jonathan Silverman, ed., *For the World to See: The Life of Margaret Bourke-White* (New York: Viking Press, 1983), p. 114.

### Chapter 2. "Reject the Easy Path!"

1. Deborah G. Felder, *The 100 Most Influential Women of All Time* (New York: Citadel Press, 1996), p. 275.

2. Margaret Bourke-White, *Portrait of Myself* (New York: Simon & Schuster, 1963), p. 18.

3. Roger White letter to Margaret Bourke-White, July 5, 1932, as cited by Vicki Goldberg, *Margaret Bourke-White: A Biography* (New York: Harper & Row, Publishers, 1986), p. 8.

4. Bourke-White, p. 22.

5. Goldberg, p. 11.

6. Bourke-White, p. 13.

7. Ibid.

8. Paul Beckley, "Lady with a Lens," *Scholastic,* October 28, 1953, p. 4.

9. Bourke-White, p. 18.

10. Ibid., p. 14.

11. Ibid., pp. 23–24.

## Chapter 3. Rough Waters

1. Deborah G. Felder, *The 100 Most Influential Women of All Time* (New York: Citadel Press, 1996), p. 275.

2. Margaret Bourke-White, typescript, n.d., as cited by Vicki Goldberg, *Margaret Bourke-White: A Biography* (New York: Harper & Row, Publishers, 1986), p. 24.

3. James Enyeart, ed., *Decade by Decade, Twentieth-Century American Photography* (Boston: Bulfinch Press, 1989), p. 20.

4. Margaret Bourke-White, typescript, n.d., as cited by Goldberg, p. 26.

5. Goldberg, pp. 27–28.

6. Ibid., pp. 31–32.

7. Margaret Bourke-White, *Portrait of Myself* (New York: Simon & Schuster, 1963), p. 25.

8. Ibid.

9. Goldberg, pp. 36–37.

10. Bourke-White, pp. 27–28.

11. Ibid., p. 28.

12. Ibid.

13. T. Otto Hall, "The Camera Is a Candid Machine," *Scholastic,* May 15, 1937, p. 18.

14. Bourke-White, p. 30.

15. Helen McLean Sprackling, "Child of Adventure," *Pictorial Review,* December 1934, p. 62.

## Chapter 4.  A Career Is Launched

1. Vicki Goldberg, *Margaret Bourke-White: A Biography* (New York: Harper & Row, Publishers, 1986), p. 87.

2. Marjorie Talalay, *Margaret Bourke-White, The Cleveland Years, 1927–1930* (Cleveland: New Gallery of Contemporary Art, 1976), p. iii.

3. Margaret Bourke-White, *Portrait of Myself* (New York: Simon & Schuster, 1963), p. 38.

4. Talalay, p. iii.

5. T. Otto Hall, "The Camera Is a Candid Machine," *Scholastic,* May 15, 1937, p. 18.

6. Margaret Bourke-White, *Eyes on Russia* (New York: AMS Press, 1931), p. 65.

7. Edna Robb Webster, "This Daring Camera Girl Scales Skyscrapers for Art," *American Magazine,* November 1930, p. 66.

8. Talalay, p. iii.

9. Ibid., pp. iii–iv.

10. Bourke-White, *Portrait of Myself,* pp. 33–34.

11. Ibid., p. 49.

12. Ibid.

13. Margaret Bourke-White, "Photographing This World," *Nation,* February 19, 1936, p. 217.

14. NEA Magazine, 1929, Margaret Bourke-White Collection, as cited by Goldberg, p. 93.

15. Talalay, p. iv.

16. Bourke-White, *Portrait of Myself,* p. 60.

17. Jonathan Silverman, ed., *For the World to See: The Life of Margaret Bourke-White* (New York: Viking Press, 1983), p. 9.

18. Ibid., p. 10.

## Chapter 5.  Fame with Fortune

1. Jonathan Silverman, ed., *For the World to See: The Life of Margaret Bourke-White* (New York: Viking Press, 1983), p. 10.

2. Ibid.

3. Ibid.

4. Margaret Bourke-White, *Portrait of Myself* (New York: Simon & Schuster, 1963), p. 63.

5. Ibid., p. 70.

6. Ibid., p. 71.

7. Vicki Goldberg, *Margaret Bourke-White: A Biography* (New York: Harper & Row, Publishers, 1986), p. 115.

8. Silverman, p. 8.

## Chapter 6.  Pictures from Russia

1. Jonathan Silverman, ed., *For the World to See: The Life of Margaret Bourke-White* (New York: Viking Press, 1983), p. 28.

2. Margaret Bourke-White, *Eyes on Russia* (New York: AMS Press, 1931), p. 23.

3. Silverman, p. 28.

4. Margaret Bourke-White, *Portrait of Myself* (New York: Simon & Schuster, 1963), p. 90.

5. Ibid., p. 92.

6. Bourke-White, *Eyes on Russia,* p. 28.

7. Bourke-White, *Portrait of Myself,* p. 93.

8. Bourke-White, *Eyes on Russia,* p. 38.

9. Ibid., p. 74.

10. Ibid., p. 13.

11. Ibid., p. 132.

12. Ibid.

13. Vicki Goldberg, *Margaret Bourke-White: A Biography* (New York: Harper & Row, Publishers, 1986), pp. 130–131.

14. Ibid., p. 136.

## Chapter 7. Shifting Focus

1. William Stott, *Documentary Expression and Thirties America* (New York: Oxford University Press, 1973), pp. 71-72.

2. Ibid., p. 3.

3. Vicki Goldberg, *Margaret Bourke-White: A Biography* (New York: Harper & Row, Publishers, 1986), p. 153.

4. Ibid., p. 131.

5. Margaret Bourke-White, "Dust Changes America," *Nation,* May 22, 1935, p. 597.

6. Jonathan Silverman, ed., *For the World to See: The Life of Margaret Bourke-White* (New York: Viking Press, 1983), p. 75.

7. T. Otto Hall, "The Camera Is a Candid Machine," *Scholastic,* May 15, 1937, p. 19.

8. Silverman, p. 79.

9. Ibid., p. 74.

10. Electa Clark, *Leading Ladies* (New York: Stein and Day, 1972), p. 148.

11. Undated letter postmarked July 26, 1936, Erskine Caldwell Collection, Dartmouth College Library, as cited by Goldberg, p. 166.

12. Goldberg, p. 168.

13. Erskine Caldwell and Margaret Bourke-White, *You Have Seen Their Faces* (New York: Modern Age Books, Inc.,1937), p. 51.

14. Ibid., p. 2.

15. Stott, p. 214.

16. Harvey L. Klevar, *Erskine Caldwell: A Biography* (Knoxville: University of Tennessee Press, 1993), p. 201.

## Chapter 8. A Passion for Pictures

1. Vicki Goldberg, *Margaret Bourke-White: A Biography* (New York: Harper & Row, Publishers, 1986), p. 174.

2. Jonathan Silverman, ed., *For the World to See: The Life of Margaret Bourke-White* (New York: Viking Press, 1983), p. 81.

3. Loudon Wainwright, "Life Begins," *Atlantic Monthly,* May 1970, p. 69.

4. "Introduction," *Life,* November 23, 1936.

5. Wainwright, p. 70.

6. Goldberg, p. 188.

7. Wainwright, p. 73.

8. Edna Robb Webster, "This Daring Camera Girl Scales Skyscrapers for Art," *American Magazine,* November 1930, p. 69.

9. Goldberg, p. 197.

10. Harvey L. Klevar, *Erskine Caldwell: A Biography* (Knoxville: University of Tennessee Press, 1993), p. 184.

11. Margaret Bourke-White, *Portrait of Myself* (New York: Simon & Schuster, 1963), p. 170.

12. Ibid., p. 171.

13. Silverman, p. 107.

### Chapter 9.  Dodging Bombs

1. Margaret Bourke-White and Jonathan Silverman, ed., *The Taste of War* (London: Century Publishing, 1942), pp. 34–35.

2. Erskine Caldwell, *With All My Might* (Atlanta: Peachtree Publishers, 1987), p. 186.

3. Bourke-White and Silverman, p. 56.

4. Ibid., p. 49.

5. Jonathan Silverman, ed., *For the World to See: the Life of Margaret Bourke-White* (New York: Viking Press, 1983), p. 109.

6. Bourke-White and Silverman, p. 65.

7. Caldwell, p. 201.

8. Bourke-White, *Portrait of Myself,* p. 197.

9. Ibid., p. 226.

10. Bourke-White and Silverman, p. 146.

11. Ibid.

12. Ibid., p. 152.

13. Silverman, p. 121.

14. Bourke-White, *Portrait of Myself,* p. 234.

15. David A. Hackett, trans., *The Buchenwald Report* (Boulder, Colo.: Westview Press, 1995), p. 99.

16. Carlo D'este, *Patton, A Genius for War* (New York: HarperCollins Publishers, 1995), pp. 720–721.

17. Sean Callahan, ed., *The Photographs of Margaret Bourke-White* (New York: Bonanza Books, 1972), p. 141.

18. Ibid., pp. 152–153.

19. Bourke-White, *Portrait of Myself,* p. 260.

## Chapter 10. The Toughest Challenge

1. Jonathan Silverman, ed., *For the World to See: The Life of Margaret Bourke-White* (New York: Viking Press, 1983), p. 175.

2. Margaret Bourke-White, *Portrait of Myself* (New York: Simon & Schuster, 1963), p. 315.

3. Silverman, p. 187.

4. Ibid., p. 188.

5. Ibid., p. 190.

6. Bourke-White, p. 368.

7. Margaret Bourke-White, "Famous Lady's Indomitable Fight," *Life,* June 22, 1959, p. 103.

8. Les Barry, "What About the Future?" *Popular Photography,* June 1960, p. 105.

9. "Margaret Bourke-White," *Life,* September 10, 1971, p. 34.

10. Deborah G. Felder, *The 100 Most Influential Women of All Time* (New York: Citadel Press, 1996), p. 277.

11. "Bourke-White's 25 Years," *Life,* May 16, 1955, p. 16.

12. Felder, p. 277.

# Further Reading

Bourke-White, Margaret. *Portrait of Myself.* New York: Simon & Schuster, 1963.

Bourke-White, Margaret, and Jonathan Silverman, ed. *The Taste of War.* London: Century Publishing, 1985.

Caldwell, Erskine, and Margaret Bourke-White. *You Have Seen Their Faces.* New York: Viking Press, 1937.

Callahan, Sean, ed. *Margaret Bourke-White, Photographer.* New York: Little, Brown and Company, 1988.

Daffron, Carolyn. *Margaret Bourke-White.* New York: Chelsea House Publishers, 1988.

Keller, Emily. *Margaret Bourke-White: A Photographer's Life.* Minneapolis: Lerner Publishing Company, 1996.

Rubin, Susan Goldman. *Margaret Bourke-White: Her Pictures Were Her Life.* New York: Harry N. Abrams, 1999.

Siegel, Beatrice. *An Eye on the World: Margaret Bourke-White, Photographer.* New York: Frederick Warne, 1980.

## Internet Addresses

**Women in History: Portrait and Biography**
<http://www.lkwdpl.org/wihohio/bour-mar.htm>

**Banning and Associates: Nine Bourke-White Photographs**
<http://photoarts.com/banning/gallery/bourkewhite.html>

**Lessons in Looking: Biography, lessons, and resources on the history of photography.**
<http://www.efn.org/~sroehr/mbwindex.html>

# Index

Page numbers for photographs are in **boldface** type.

Frances Harper Junior High School
4000 East Covell Blvd.
Davis, CA 95618